THE ARTS IN THE
CLASSROOM

NATALIE ROBINSON COLE

THE ARTS IN THE CLASSROOM

WITH PHOTOGRAPHS BY C. K. EATON

THE JOHN DAY COMPANY · NEW YORK

To my husband
HARRY ALBERT COLE

PREFACE

A long time ago, one Robert Browning pointed out the contrast between "allowing the imprisoned glory to escape" and imposing one's ideas upon another person. In no field has this been more true than in the field of the representative arts. You can secure one type of reaction by a curriculum rigidly directed from without or you can release children and adults so that creative activity occurs spontaneously and inevitably.

Mrs. Cole is a teacher who professes belief in Browning's dictum and acts upon it in a practical and effective way with her children. This book shows how an intelligent, sympathetic, and kindly teacher released the creative spirit in her pupils and secured results which are almost unbelievable. Mrs. Cole's techniques, as related herewith, will be a continued inspiration to the reader, whether he be professional teacher, parent, or interested layman.

ROBERT HILL LANE

CONTENTS

ILLUSTRATIONS

Author's Foreword

The material of this book was contributed by a group of nine-, ten-, and eleven-year-old children during their fourth grade and first half of the fifth at California Street School, Los Angeles. Half of the group were Mexican, a quarter Chinese, and the rest Japanese and American. Their I.Q.'s would have consigned many of them to a rather meager existence, but I found plenty to work with and felt they stopped only where I stopped in my ability and understanding.

I wish to express my very great appreciation to Mrs. Mildred Hayes, Principal, for giving me confidence in my own way of teaching; Mr. Herman Sachs, whose generous recognition of my children's art work gave me my first impetus to write this book; Miss Rosemary Livsey, head of the School and Teachers' Department, Los Angeles Public Library, who read my manuscript through its many stages and counseled me in every way; Mr. Robert Hill Lane, Assistant Superintendent of Schools, Los Angeles; and Dr. A. Gordon Melvin, College of the City of New York, for their encouragement and very real help; and Miss Gertrude Copley, whose beautiful work in children's creative dancing has been my inspiration.

I also thank my friend, Miss Julia Taylor, for proofreading, and my photographer, Mr. C. K. Eaton, for his patience and skill.

1. Creative Painting

Children cannot create out of a vacuum. They must have something to say and be fired to say it. More time spent in experiencing richly what they are going to paint will bear fruit in faster outpouring of the child's picture when he gets started.

If anybody thinks teaching children's painting is a negative job, with the teacher sitting at her desk while the children jump at the chance to "paint anything you want to, boys and girls," he is all wrong. He will very likely find that most of the children don't want to paint anything very much and those who do seem to want to hash over a picture they made in some former room at an earlier time.

Need of Discussion and Build-up

I tried this "paint what you'd like to for Christmas" one time and was surprised to get back almost as many great, ugly brick fireplaces as there were children in the room, with every brick painted in individually and a feeble show of Christmas gifts on top. There had been no discussion, no build-up. There was a poverty of experience. The children took refuge in the safe harbor of a good old dictated picture from "away back." Everyone has seen the child drawing the absolutely sterile house with curtains tied at each side of the windows. The

3

child must have his mind and emotions aroused about something and want to paint before he will paint well.

Every group must reach out for its own live experiences. Is there a barber shop near by, or a bakery? Are men tearing down the buildings or tearing up the street? Are there great trucks, electric drills, or steam shovels in the neighborhood? Are there roofers at work with their caldron of tar? Is there a program or a track meet? Would the kindergarten or nursery let the group come for a few minutes?

Can You Paint a Street Car?

Years ago I took a group of children across the street to a macaroni factory. They came back and painted what they saw. It was unbelievable. From their mind's eye they put on paper the huge mixing vats, the complicated belt system—and put it in motion, if you please; the strings of dough oozing out of the sieve-like openings; the great lengths of it on drying racks; the electric switches and gadgets on the walls—even the exact words the workers had been saying.

Try to imagine yourself or some other adult starting out to paint the same subject. Picture your absolute fear and impotence. The child surmounts all difficulty, portrays the most complicated things without blinking an eye. For instance, here's an easy one. Every child can paint a street car. Can you? He may eliminate all the nonessentials, but he will have the elements that distinguish it, and the trolley wire that makes it go.

We Go Places

Suppose we go to the school cafeteria and then come back to paint a picture. The children are beginning the fourth grade and are from nine to eleven years of age. They are

A child's picture travels on its interest.

From among the most timid will come some of the finest painter

largely Mexican and Chinese with a handful of Japanese and American. First the teacher asks the children why they are going. The children answer, "To get our eyes full." She tells them to look well, reminding them that some people have been known to go places and see only their feet or what they take along with them.

Now, it is not necessary actually to go to the cafeteria. Children can paint from their own minds the school cafeteria, the circus, traffic, or anything else within their line of interest —entirely independent of having seen it near the time of painting.

But, although it isn't necessary, it does help their interest, and we know that a child's picture travels on its interest.

The subject should be made so interesting that the child is just bursting to put it on paper. When the child is full of ideas, his picture will spill out somehow. The teacher's job is to help keep it coming by giving praise and encouragement.

How to Get Going

The teacher says, for instance, "Well, here's a brave fellow. He's not going to take all day to get started. See how he is putting in the workers, big and strong. He knows he can tuck in the other things later.

"My, what a fine stove Teruo has! How clever of him to remember just how those pipes go up. I suppose he's going to put Mrs. Johnson taking out the pies.

"See how Helen Quan has painted Miss Black. She's watching to see that the children take a hot dish. How many of you have been in her kindergarten?"

"I have!" . . . . "I have!" . . . . "I have!" . . . .

"Then you'll make her picture very fine indeed.

"Now everybody's getting a good start. Fine, Ernest! Fine, Manuel! What a lot of swing, Alicia!"

Recognize Quickly

A teacher should train herself to recognize quickly what the child is portraying; she should never, under any circumstances, confess that she is stumped and must make inquiry.

Sometimes a child is so afraid that the teacher will not recognize what he is painting that he will shield it with his hand rather than expose it to a nonunderstanding, unsympathetic eye.

As the child finds that the teacher feels he has good ideas and the ability to express them, his whole attitude changes and relaxes. We see him welcome the teacher's gaze until he will beg of her, "Please, come take a look at my peecture."

It will go along something like this:

"See, I make Mrs. Johnson saying, 'Help! Help! It's burning!' "

And the teacher says, "Oh, that's why her arms are thrown up in the air. No wonder she's excited."

One after another the children say, "I make the teakettle say, 'Choo-choo-choo. . . !' You know, like it sounds when it's boiling."

"I make a clock so Mrs. Johnson will know when the children are coming."

"I make Mrs. Cole. See, I make your picture. I put the dress you have on. You don't care if you are fat. My mother is fat too."

"I paint a kettle of soup and when I see it in the picture, it makes me hungry."

"I put lots of bottles of milk 5¢ because it's good for you."

"I make the cash register. She says, 'Ten cents, please!' See, I make it say 10¢."

"Make It Your Own Way"

The teacher should watch for the child with a very individual way of making his figures and things. From him will come the pictures of character and distinction. She should never try to show him how the human figure actually is, but rather build up his strength and surety.

"Make your picture your own way, Teresa. Don't ever try to paint like anyone else. We want to be able to look at your picture and say, 'That's Teresa's picture.' "

The teacher should go about, lifting one picture after another, giving some appreciation. It doesn't matter that many children will not lift their eyes from their own painting. What the teacher says goes in their mind's ear, and they will strive to do as much or better.

In watching the new child in the room we can see that fear and lack of faith hold him back far more than any lack of native ability.

When I came to this school I started to paint, but I said, "This brush is not good and there is no red." I was still fussing when it was time to stop. When I painted it was too much like a copy picture and it was too small. The teacher said, "It isn't your real picture. Don't be afraid, just do it as you want." I thought I shouldn't be a cream puff. I should make it my own way. So I started with a big fat brush and I made a big picture. Then the teacher said, "I told you so."

From among the most timid will come some of the finest painters. The timid child is apt to be the most creative child, the one most sensitive to beauty.

Confidence and Respect

The teacher should give the children a confidence and respect for their painting as children's painting.

"It's wonderful the way you children can start right out and paint anything. You don't worry and stew around like grown-ups. You just go ahead and paint it. Grown-ups would be fussing around about how to paint one little thing while you have the whole picture painted beautifully.

"Children can paint pictures that 'feel' like the thing they're painting. Any little old camera can take pictures of things as they really look."

Later they will say, "He shouldn't try to paint like grown-ups, should he? He should paint it his own way." Children are intelligent. They can grasp truths that we adults stumble over.

A Picture Unfolds

A good picture is like a birth. It unfolds and is not forced. A teacher can't force fine painting down children's throats. She must be content to open them up by getting and holding their liking and respect. Good children's painting comes as a result of a rapport established and the feeling that the teacher has faith that they can do it.

Hands Off

The teacher should never seek to help a child by taking the brush in hand to show him how something ought to be. She should never attempt to show on the blackboard or by photographs or pictures how something really is.

The fact that the teacher cannot draw the proverbial straight line encourages us to hope that she will not attempt to impose her own adult way of doing or try to pull the brush from the child's tightly clenched fist to add or guide a bit.

The child has a marvelous ability to express himself. If properly drawn out and encouraged, he needs no help. The moment a teacher draws on the board or paints on paper, that moment is the child crippled and inhibited. That moment is he ruined for confidence in his own way of doing. Hands off!

Children's Own Proportions

The teacher should respect the child's own proportions. He should be allowed his own interpretation of the relative size of things in the picture without any reference to their actual size.

The little child works as a primitive, with no compulsion to follow the actual appearance and proportions of people and things. He has a fascinating way of putting the things most important to him in largest, while the less significant things are either deleted entirely or given little room and attention.

There is a story of an experiment in which some Russian professors had children paint the inside of a peasant's hut. The great stove, that contributed so much in that bleak northland, the children made so large as to nearly fill the picture.

The professors studied the children's various interpretations figuring everything until they came to one picture with a great oval in its center. This oval was filled with dynamic crisscross marks and was a third as big as the giant stove.

Finally one professor caught it: they were the matches . . . without which the stove would be cold and life unbearable. Very likely, too, matches at that time, in that country, were not so taken for granted as they are here and now. The child had only accorded them the attention he felt they deserved.

This capacity for unconscious distortion the teacher will find one of the charming features of children's art, one of the unexpected twists that only the child mind could conceive.

Effort Worth While

Children have genius—yes. But the teacher must dig to get at it. Gold is seldom found for the idle taking. The tools here are praise and encouragement. That this is worth while can be proved readily. Because the wonderful truth is that, as the teacher digs down and removes layers of frustration and defeat and gives the child the faith and confidence to express himself in painting, she is helping to give him confidence to express himself creatively in many ways.

The child is freed to express himself in words. If the teacher listens she will hear, "I'd like to work in the cafeteria. I'd scrub the pans all nice and clean. I do that at home every day at my house."

"Yesterday I saw a little boy lick his fingers from the smallest to the biggest."

"That's funny. We paint a picture about the cafeteria, then we go there and eat."

"If we didn't have a cafeteria we would go down to the corner and buy hot dogs and Pepsi-Cola. Your mother don't worry if you eat at the cafeteria."

"My mother scolded me because I said buy lunch. She said, 'You think we got enough money to buy lunch for you?'"

"I don't know why some children that eat free lunch they

leave their lunch on the table just because they don't like it. My little brother and me have to eat everything they give us because we don't want to have my mother worry about us. Sometimes my little brother doesn't want to eat something, so I tell him, 'You have to eat it.' My mother says every day, 'You eat everything they give you. You eat every bit of it. If you don't like it anyway you have to eat it.' "

"One day I spill my tray. I spill my cup of soup and dish of mashed potatoes. I was so sad. But they gave me another cup of soup and dish of mashed potatoes. Then I was happy again."

"Just like Painting, Huh?"

The children will say of making clay animals or dancing, or writing, or whatever it is they are doing, "It's just like painting, huh? You got to do it your own way. You mustn't be afraid; just feel it inside and do it."

Tools to Work With

After the child has something to say and the confidence to say it, there is still much that the teacher can do. She can give him tools to work with in the form of a few definite principles of good art, which will help him make a successful picture.

These the teacher does not propound directly but teaches through praise when they occur. In this way the child is not burdened intellectually, but learns through repetition in pleasant association.

These principles are simple and easy for the teacher to grasp. There is no specialized art language or understanding necessary.

Should Be Big

In the first place, children's painting should be big. This is the way children work naturally. It gives them physical satisfaction and puts little strain on eyes and nerves. I once heard of a teacher having children paint from far out on a ladder to compel large, free body movement.

All too often children have been allowed to draw with pencil on small pieces of paper. Many times this becomes not a satisfactory emotional experience, but a very bad nervous habit—an escape from reality.

If painting is a worth-while activity, it is worthy of an 18″ × 24″ piece of paper. This size painting lends itself to our modern homes and the school wall spaces. As the child says, "If it isn't big you can't see it."

Bump the Sides

True, just passing out a large sheet of paper will not guarantee large, free painting. A little conscious attention at this point can save a lot of bad beginnings.

Let us continue with the cafeteria picture idea. The teacher says, "I wonder just how big this paper will let us paint? Come here, Dora, let us see."

We hold the paper against her back and find there is room to spare.

"Well," the teacher says, "of course Dora is about the smallest girl we have, but how many of you think we could make Mrs. Johnson as big as Dora and still have room to tuck in our stoves and other things? . . . Fine! Now show me how big you will make Mrs. Johnson. . . . That's a promise. Don't let us see any little stingy, 'fraidy cat' pictures. Make your picture fill your paper till it bumps the sides."

At the first sign of some child painting something big and strong, the teacher should hold it up and praise it. It doesn't matter whether it's terribly good or not. If it isn't so good, that in itself will encourage others who know they can do better.

Beginning Outline

Next, I believe that beginning with an outline makes painting easy for the teacher as well as the child. It's the way of early man on his cave wall—it's the way of children on sidewalk and fence. This outline can be of any color—however, mixing a little black with their outline color will give a more satisfying light and dark to the picture. This outline should carry over from one edge of the paper to the other, and from top to bottom. Curving over one part of the child's paper and showing it by itself is a good way of convincing him that it "needs something else there."

If the child paints his whole picture first in outline, he can concentrate on what he has to say and get out something that is really worth coloring later.

Holding off the rest of the colors acts as an incentive toward pushing him through the more difficult organization end of his picture. Soon there are no poky children.

When the teacher sees this line phase well done, the child may start with his other color. The picture by this time is so well begun that the child finds it easy to finish successfully. This is a case of limiting the child to free the child. Children accept this way of doing and are quick to realize that it is fair and wise.

I have found in my own experience that without this beginning outline ofttimes the child will jump from one color

to another, painting at little individual things and giving little
or no attention to the whole idea of the picture.

His picture is apt to lag and fall by the wayside, long
before it is finished. The rhythmic flow of his space filling
will be severed by his stopping to shift colors.

The teacher should be most active, praising with all her
might those who are painting strongly and freely, and encouraging the others away from the little, tight, fussy, copy-
type of thing.

Children Pass Judgment

Suppose we let the children decide how things are going.

"I'm through! I'm through!" says Ernesto.

"Children, Ernesto says he's through. What do you
think?"

"No. He hasn't enough things happening."

"He has to weave some more people in."

"It's too dishwatery. He needs stronger color."

"It's too fussy. He worries too much."

"It's too dead. He paints too slow."

"I think it's pretty good. He just came here a while back."

"I think like Lucille," says the teacher. "It's pretty good.
Of course, he is a little bit too careful. But then we all were
when we first started. Maybe he could put the man grinding
carrots and the boys washing trays. And what a splendid
place he has for the cash register."

True, some of the kids didn't like his picture, but teacher
has stuck up for him. And shucks, if they want it bigger and
stronger he can make it that way too. It's lots easier than
making it careful and just like real. Anyway, he's got a couple
of good ideas. So he starts out again, quite pleased with himself.

Color

Children have their own dynamic way of using color. They have taught me many things . . . that color should be strong, even as life itself is strong. Sometimes they mix their skin color of yellow with tiny bits of orange and purple. This helps give a chance for much warm color. If the other large areas are warm, then all the child has to do to get a satisfying color effect is to add a minimum of cool color in the small bits here and there. Sometimes he will reverse this by making the skin his minimum of warm color and the large balance of his picture cool. Jesus' "Street Scene," opposite page 101, was done this latter way.

We find children "distributing" their color throughout the picture. The teacher can help by suggesting indirectly, "Hilda has a fine red dress on Mrs. Johnson. What shall she remember to do?"

"Find some other place to put the red."

"Put it around the stove and the signs."

"It don't matter what color it really is. We put it the way we want. It's our picture, isn't it? Well, so why not?"

Sometimes children, by using the dirty water in the jar to mix their paints, take the bright edge off the colors, giving a very different feeling all by accident.

A little of this dirty water painted around the outside of things in the picture helps to tie it together and gives a feeling of unity and depth.

"Weaving-in" Process

Then there is a "weaving-in" process. A picture is better looking if it is not all spread out equally. Things tucked in behind give depth and interest to the picture.

"This is a fine 'woven-in' picture," the teacher says to the children. "See how he's tucked things in behind, weaving them to fill the space."

Children Call It "Swing"

Now a word about rhythm—children call it "swing."

The teacher says, "See how John 'pulls' his things the same way. We like to feel the 'pull' in his picture."

Or, "See how Alicia makes Mrs. Johnson's back swing across the paper. She makes the steam table swing the same way."

Just as freeing the children through painting has helped make joyous dancing possible, so has dancing contributed to their painting, giving increased rhythm.

Also, there is the rhythm of repeated form.

The teacher says, "Look at Teruo's picture. See how he uses the same pattern for all his cafeteria workers. That gives us 'repetition,' and we like it."

Jesus, using the same pattern for his baby buggy and for his tamale wagon in his "Street Scene" picture, again gives us a good example.

Alicia, in her picture, "I'm Proud I Am a Safety," shows us both rhythm and repetition. The upraised arms give a rhythmic flow, while the faces in the window are repeated in the waiting line below.

Going Again

Now, to almost every child there comes a let-down somewhere in the course of his picture. His first burst of creative activity is over. His picture is only partly done, his space poorly filled. Yet he settles down with a satisfied air. How to get him going again is the question.

Let us take Manuel. Manuel has only three children in his cafeteria line. They are so small that it will take twelve or fifteen to give his line proper weight and balance. He has very evidently stopped.

The teacher does not begin by telling Manuel to stop wasting his time or to look at Jesus, who has almost finished his picture. She begins by complimenting him on what he has been painting.

She says, "What a fine refrigerator Manuel has! Now he is starting to put in his children. I wonder how many children are in that line at noon time."

"I think about fifty" . . . . "I think about a hundred," the children answer.

"Well," says the teacher, "if there are so many we had better get busy and all work fast."

Manuel sees that the teacher doesn't understand that his picture is finished—that he quit long ago. She thinks he is still going strong. She likes what he's been doing. He can't break faith with the teacher, so he starts again. He fills in more children and saves his picture.

Because he has pushed himself through this picture, the next one will come easier.

"I Spoiled Mine"

Then there is the "I spoiled mine!" that every teacher has to deal with.

"I spoiled mine! I spoiled mine!" the child shouts triumphantly across the room.

"Well," the teacher says calmly, "keep it a secret. Don't make us unhappy about it. A smart painter never spoils anything anyway."

And from the children, "Sure, little things don't matter,

do they? It's whether you got something happening. He can just paint on top of that. Nobody'll care, huh?"

Where there is no sympathy and attention accorded, the "I spoiled mine" children grow fewer and fewer.

I told the teacher I spoiled my picture. Then she said, "You children get the funniest ideas about what spoils pictures. Listen to me, those little things don't hurt. The only thing that spoils a picture is not to make it your own way."

Then Carmen, my best friend, said, "I spoiled mine, Ofelia." And I said, "Don't worry, Carmen, for you didn't."

Step Out of the Picture

Whenever possible the teacher should step out of the picture and let the children handle their own situations. She will find the job better done than if she handled it herself.

Roberto says, "I feenish! I feenish!" The teacher looks and says, "How many think this is a good picture for Roberto, after we've been letting him go early every day to help out at the cafeteria?"

No answer.

Roberto, rising to his defense, says, "Yeah, but I don't go to look. I go to work."

At this Alicia says, "He can show what he work, huh? What you work, Roberto? You paint it in the picture."

Although the child has begun by painting communal subjects, later a word or two from the teacher will start him illustrating his own life stories from the writing period.

Getting Ready

Proper mounting and display can add one hundred per cent to the child's picture and have its corresponding effect on the child.

But first let us look to see if we are ready. Does his "Street Scene" picture have a weak edge all around where it fails to "bump the sides"? Trimming the weak edges adds strength immediately. Is the child's Father picture noticeably off balance, being too much to the side? Trimming from the one side sets his father squarely in the middle.

This doesn't mean for a moment that the teacher is to depend on the paper cutter for fine space-filling. She will stress beautiful space-filling always. And many of these weaknesses will be caught during the painting lesson. Later the teacher will find some children filling space so masterfully that their picture will not stand trimming a quarter of an inch. Maria's Madonna (opposite page 5) filled the space this way.

And I don't mean every figure must be set squarely in the middle. Children have their own amazing way of balancing a picture that starts off center, even if they have to hook an arm three times the length of the other down and up to fill the space.

But there are times when trimming will do much to bring out the character and distinction that the child's picture undeniably has.

Mounting

The easiest and most effective way of mounting these large pictures is to put them against black mounting paper so the black shows a quarter of an inch all around. Then put them against tag-board, size 22" × 28½". The tiny black edge ties the picture with its strong dark and light together. The broad border of off-white tag-board gives a most beautiful modern effect.

Display

After the pictures are made ready with their mountings, the question is where to put them to advantage. In this the teacher will follow the modern trend in decoration by putting them on the eye level. If this space is already occupied by framed pictures, perhaps the teacher could gather courage to remove them. It means little to these artists whether their pictures are hung or not. It means a lot to the child.

The teacher should be careful that the effect of the children's pictures is not nullified by the room having too many distracting doodads, picture calendars, and other meaningless matter. The teacher should give the children's pictures a chance to make the room sing with their glory. Then every painting lesson will go easier and better than the one before. After every painting time the children's pictures can be changed. The finest of the old may be saved for room and school exhibits. Outstanding recognition given fine work is better than a thousand words.

"Child with Problems"

The teacher can use creative painting to help the problem child, or "child with problems" as we are admonished now to say.

She will feel her tiredness leave like magic when she sees a picture well done, and mounts it for all the world to see that Johnny isn't the "pain-in-the-neck" that the world, and, most unfortunately, Johnny himself have been thinking. What this child's underlying difficulty may be, a teacher with a roomful can hardly determine readily. But ten to one, whatever it is, he's trying to convince himself and the world that he's Somebody. He's so shaky, so insecure within that he has

"I'm Proud I Am a Safety."

Tangible proof that he is a worth-while perso

to be calling for attention to sustain himself. It matters not whether the attention is favorable or otherwise.

Now, properly interested, even the problem child likes to paint. If through the power of suggestion or some other means the teacher can get the child to make a good picture, she has made a big start. She can confront him with the tangible proof that he is a worth-while person, able to make a worth-while contribution.

The teacher can prove her faith in him and his picture by mounting it handsomely and putting it alone on a great wall space for him and all to see. As long as it remains, there is the constant reminder that he is a very fine person or he couldn't have made such a picture. The proof is on the wall.

If the teacher can print a name plate and put it under his picture, so there's no mistaking, the job is so much furthered. Constant reference to his picture in one connection or another helps the idea to sink in.

I have watched a child actually keep the corner of his eye turned on his picture a good part of the day, his efforts to show unconcern to the contrary. But having his mind off his lessons didn't bother me a bit. I knew that this was the one great lesson he needed to learn; that he was an all-right sort of person; that he was accepted and so didn't have to worry any more about his place among us. What this can do for the problem child it can do for all children.

Water-color painting in the classroom isn't easy. At the beginning things can happen one after another, enough to try a saint, let alone a half-worn-down teacher. Water is spilled, brushes disappear or are exchanged. I remember some child walking unconcernedly across a whole row of pictures, and others, deliberately and with malice aforethought, splattering someone else's painting. However, the teacher's irritation and fatigue at this stage are little alongside the children's opportunity for joy and growth.

How It Works

For instance, it can work as follows: Ming Chan breaks out excitedly, "Teruo kicked the water all over my picture! Yes you did! You did too! I see him do it!"

To Ming this is no less than an echo of the great Sino-Japanese conflict.

"Quiet, Ming!" the teacher says. "How about it, children? Teruo says he's sorry and didn't mean to do it. What shall Ming do?"

"Take a blotter and forget about it," says someone. "Don't fuss. Life's too short, like Dr. Dolittle says."

Ofelia calls: "I'm done! I'm done! I'm tired painting. I don't want to paint any more."

"What shall we say to Ofelia, children?"

"Well, her picture isn't done. We can tell her that much. But if she doesn't want to paint any more, she won't paint no good anyway."

"Let her sit down and take a book and don't bother the rest of us."

Ernest says, "I need a steef brush, like Jesus have. I cannot paint good with this soft brush."

The children say, "There aren't any more. You'll have to wait till someone finish."

"He'll use the soft brush. He can paint a good picture with any kind of brush if he try hard enough."

"He can take mine for a while. I like to use the other one."

Surely, children's creative painting provides opportunity to test out all the virtues of unselfishness, thoughtfulness, dependability, stick-to-itiveness, patience, cleanliness, Godliness, and whatever else we're aiming at in the school program of today.

New Rapport

No, water-color painting is not a good thing to do on the side while the teacher is figuring her register, but if she gives it her wholehearted interest, it can be a grand, enriching experience for both herself and the children. It will put beautiful, modern paintings on the walls, which will stretch out to the halls and office and the children's homes. It can be the means through which a new rapport between teacher and children is established, that will help her in anything else she wants to do. It's a good way to get acquainted with the child mind and to learn to speak his language.

In Conclusion

The teacher should remember that the growing process is more important than the end product—the child more important than the picture.

I like to paint because as I told you before, it is fun. And if you want a good picture you have to work hard on it and feel it inside and keep working with it and take pains with it and make it strong and don't be looking around or talking to anyone and mind your own business and don't be running around.

Then you can make a good picture and the teacher will hang it out in the hall and you will have something to be proud of.

If the teacher gives the children a confidence and respect and love for painting, everything else will follow as the night follows the day.

"I told my mother if I could go to school and she said 'No, because you still are sick,' And I said, 'But mother, I got to go because maybe the children are painting pictures.'"

"Everybody could make a good picture if they tried, couldn't they? I bet Mrs. Cole could make a good picture if she wanted to. Huh, Mrs. Cole, huh?"

And then from some child, in dreamy fashion:

"I love to paint. I would like to paint every hour, every day. I never get tired painting."

2. Creative Clay Work

Working with clay is another thrilling way to watch the child unfold and to learn his language. Here again background is not necessary. It is the love and understanding in the teacher's heart, not the ability in her hands, that counts.

Working with clay answers a definite need in the emotional life of the child. When we add to the squeezing and squashing and mixing and rolling, the joy that comes from creating something beautiful, we are providing emotional satisfaction indeed.

Clay Is Messy

Children love clay. Psychologists are strong for it. The only stickler seems to be that clay is messy.

Yes, clay *is* messy by its very nature. But if we accept that clay is good, we must accept the mess attending. An emasculated clay program where the emphasis is put on everything being kept spick and span will bring forth little of creative value. A child or a teacher cannot serve two masters. If the teacher feels embarrassed before the principal because there is clay on the doorknobs and tracks down the hall, the fault lies with the principal, not the clay. Most important in this connection is to see that the children are so interested that they will find no time to throw bits of clay at the ceiling or at each other.

Getting Ready

Other than the conviction that mess is not important, born of soul struggle if need be, the teacher needs little else to get started.

The clay she can order dry or mixed. The mixed clay costs more, but is a great convenience. If the clay is dry, she mixes it in a crock or dish pan or anything she is lucky enough to have. Mixing leaves it much softer than it can be used at the time, so that means it should be mixed several days ahead and then left to dry out till it is malleable.

Then there is the need of getting all the air out so things won't explode in the firing kiln. This, two boys can do by slamming it against the back sidewalk. Then a couple of slam-bangs in unison by the children on their desks will complete the job.

If the teacher orders her clay ready mixed, all she has to do is open the air-proof package, lift the tarred paper lining and cut it into as many squares as there are children.

Clay twice the size of a man's fist makes a generous allotment.

Next, each child needs a paint pan of water. This is to wet his fingers to soften the clay as it grows harder. Also a little pan of "slip" is necessary to wet the end of anything the children are going to stick on to something else. "Slip" is clay mixed with water to gravy-like thickness. Children call it "the magic stickum."

Now, aside from several thicknesses of newspaper on each child's desk, the teacher is ready to begin.

How We Start

It is better in the beginning for all the children to start making the same subject. Actually very few of them will have anything in particular they will want to make anyway. The fact that they're all making the same subject doesn't mean for a moment that everyone will be making alike. There may be forty ways of making that one thing. But the teacher can watch and learn more directly. There is plenty for her to concentrate upon without having to jump from man to beast—from airplane to tanker. Also, in this way a mass enthusiasm for the thing is engendered, which will do much toward helping free the child emotionally.

The Cow's the Thing

So when the child says, "Can I make a little duck?" the teacher will be hard-hearted for a purpose and say guardedly, "Well now, I'll tell you. I know we all want to make what we want to make, but maybe for this first time it might be better for us all to make the same thing. Then we can listen and learn together.

"I had thought," she continues, "that we would like to make an animal that we all know very well—perhaps a cow."

"Sure, because he is our friend. He gives us milk."

"Because it gots some of those funny things."

"Because she got horns."

"It don't got horns! The bull got horns!"

"Well, anyway," breaks in the teacher placatingly, "I'm sure we would all know a cow if we saw one. How many different kinds of cows will we make?"

"As many as there are us," the children shout.

"And oh yes, children. Before we stick on the heads or

legs or tail, or anything, we dip the end in our little pan of slip. Then it won't fall off when it gets dry. We can dip our fingers in the water and pinch the clay soft when it starts to get scratchy. That's all there is to it. You may just start making."

"Make It Your Own Way" Again

Now the teacher's job is to go up and down the aisles, giving assurance to the timid, praising those who have made a brave start.

"My what a fine start Rafael has made already. Fine, Jesus! And Angela!"

Once in a while the teacher will come upon a stubborn case. Take Bing for instance.

"But I don't know how to make a cow," he persists, with an air of finality.

"Well, let's see," says the teacher kindly. "A cow is something with four legs to stand on and a tail to swish. And, oh yes, we mustn't forget the place for the milk," she adds delicately.

"Just make it your own way, Bing. Don't worry about it," she pleads. And not until she sees a beginning light of conquest in his eye does she leave him.

As the teacher goes about encouraging the children she is watching for that childlike something that expresses a cow more surely than anything anatomically correct.

For, needless to say, the teacher is not to be concerned that the child's cow be anatomically, biologically correct. Heaven help her to the contrary! The only biology it needs is the milk business.

Let the child make the cow his own way and he will make it "feel" like a cow. The cow that comes translated through the child will have an appealing naïveté that defies analysis. As in his painting, he will unconsciously leave out that which is nonessential to him and stress that which has interest.

From time to time the teacher smiles across the room at Bing, who didn't know how, and calls to him again, "Don't worry, Bing. Just make it your own way."

"That Something"

The teacher's job is to learn to recognize the child's work that has sincere feeling and rhythm about it. The teacher need not have the ideas—the children will have lots of them.

She finds that cows *have* horns. For all over the room horns are popping. Great horns, small horns, curving horns, and straight horns. Backs are sloping, backs are straight. Buckets appear, and bells about the neck. And here's a baby calf getting its "free lunch." Heads are all different, but nearly all suggesting a cow in some intuitive fashion.

"Now," says the teacher, not too discouragingly, "it's easy to put buckets and milking stools. But do you have a beautiful cow? That is the important thing. Have you made it strong and balanced? Have you made it swing?"

Then someone says at her elbow, "Rudolph has a good cow. He makes it swing."

The teacher looks. There it is—That Something she has been looking for. Rudolph has scooped a ditch down the back of his animal, accentuating the "pull" from its neck to its tail. She watches how with careful hand he twists the cow's head around so it can see its tail, all the while making the ditch down its back more beautiful. "Beautiful, Rudolph! Beautiful!" she exclaims, as if it were a string of precious pearls.

"That certainly is the secret," the teacher says, as she mutters happily to herself. "Don't worry. Make it your own way."

Bing Again

"Bing he's got a funny cow," interrupts one.

"Look at Bing's cow!" invites another.

"Come look at Bing's cow," persists another, and yet another.

The teacher crosses the room and holds it up amid a shriek of laughter. Bing, in deference to the cow's ladylike sisterhood, has placed the milk-bag squarely between the front legs. Finally Bing's bewildered look gives place to one of Chinese pride that he should be the one to cause such a sensation. When the teacher can be heard, she congratulates him on his cow's jolly personality.

This stroke helps loosen the crowd. If there is no censure forthcoming for so flagrant a mistake, why worry about how a cow really ought to be?

Helping Sound Construction

All the while the teacher is going about, giving praise and encouragement, she is also helping the child to see that his animal is put together soundly, and is not just a messed-up something of uncertain construction. She gives a little pressure here—shows how something is infirm there.

"Children, it should be clear how you want your pattern to be. If it isn't, your cow won't be worth bothering with. And when you see your clay getting dry and scratchy, wet your fingers and soften it a bit. Let's not keep going over it with water after it's made, though, or it will sag and lose its shape."

"I need some more water," says José.

"Well, go and get it," says his neighbor. "You're not nobody so great that everybody can be at your services."

When the children's interest begins to wane, and tiny bits of clay shoot here and there, then is time for the teacher to make one last round to try to get the most interesting things finished. A little added push is often needed. Remember the let-down in painting?

Keep Standard High

Then she should go up and down the aisles studying each child's clay thing carefully. There is much to learn. Only by exposing ourselves to children's expression can we learn to recognize and to love it.

Let the child see that his work is being intelligently appraised.

"Tony's cow has beautiful curving horns, but I'm sure the head will never stick on. . . . Better luck next time," says the teacher regretfully.

"Maria's has a jolly something about it, but the legs buckle in and are mashed together. We can't tell how they're made or where they come from.

"My! Albert's cow gives lots of good milk. But her body is so dry and scratchy."

"James has a good cow." . . . "James's cow is good," say James's loyal friends.

The teacher looks. James's cow has the proportions of a live cow, without any of its charm. It is without interest or personality. James has not yet broken away from the imitative.

"Well," says the teacher, her brow furrowed, studying

the situation, "it looks like a cow but it doesn't make us feel anything."

"No," the children say. "He makes it too much like a real cow. He makes a 'copy-cow.'"

The teacher should keep her standard high. The children will rise to it. She should accept nothing ordinary, without character. No figure is saved for more working on next time. If the child can't make something in the heat of creative enthusiasm, he can do it no good at a warmed-over period. Let him make a fresh start. He will have grown subconsciously in the meantime.

So after considerable evaluating on the part of the teacher and children, two cows are finally chosen as having that intangible something that bespeaks the child genius. The rest of the cows go "back to make more clay for next time."

Don't Be Discouraged

Now if the teacher fails to find this childlike quality the first time, she should not be discouraged. It may take another lesson or two to break the ice. Perhaps the children are still worrying about satisfying adult standards.

It will depend too, on how much time the teacher can give the lesson and the amount of enthusiasm she can summon. That is why I think such a lesson should come the first thing in the morning. An hour and a half is none too long. It need not come often.

Tired, but Triumphant

When these two cows are high on a cupboard away from chance bumping, the rest of the clay back in the jar, sprinkled over and covered with wet cloth for the next time, the pans away and the newspapers bundled with their drippings, and the floor cleaned, the teacher can give a great sigh of relief. She will find herself tired but triumphantly so. The beginning soil has been laid from which beautiful, creative things will sprout far more easily in the future. Her interest and understanding, once begun, will continue to grow. Each clay time she will feel greater and greater power as she puts eye and ear to the child and learns from him his secret.

The Morning After

Drying over night has made our two cows just right for painting. They are still wet but have firmly set. The color can take good hold. Their owners are sent to bring them carefully to a desk up front, where all can see. There the teacher opens a couple of mysterious little packages. She calls on Rudolph to measure out two tablespoonfuls of smoky gray powder, called "slip color" and mix it with about the same amount of water to make a thin gravy. Dissolving a couple of tablespoonfuls of gum arabic in a pint of mixing water will keep the color from running and make it stick better during firing.

"This gray-looking slip color," she answers the children's eyes, "will make a shiny black wherever we paint it, after it's been to the firing oven."

Then she calls See Lee to do the same with two tablespoonfuls of burnt orange slip color and to mix it well. "This," she says, "will make a yellow brick color, which, used with black, looks very handsome indeed."

The teacher lays out four small brushes, the size that are no longer in favor for water-color painting. One brush for each color for both of them. Having brushes for each color keeps the color clean and no color is wasted by having to wash the brush in between.

Then she says, "I wonder if anyone can see a third color around here?"

They move the tiny sacks about until finally one little fellow catches it. "The color of the cow. You can leave him white."

"Now See Lee and Rudolph have paint and they have brushes. What else will they need that is even more important?"

"To tell where to put the black—where to put the brick," the children shout.

"And where to leave it white," someone remembers.

No Help Wanted

"Ready, Rudolph?"

"I draw to make the face with black and the tail and the ditch down the back. The horns and the milk bag I leave white. The rest of the cow brick, with the funny little things."

"Splendid! And See Lee? What will your pattern be?"

See Lee has us all waiting breathlessly while he takes plenty of time for deep Oriental concentration, and then says deliberately, "I make the cow black, with brick hair down the tail, and the little end. I make white eye and milk bag—and teeth," he adds, with a master stroke.

No help solicited or wanted here.

Tom Sawyer with his fence had nothing on the power and prestige of these two.

"Many times," says the teacher, "we can't tell just how we want to paint it before we start. We do better to 'feel' our way as we go along."

Successful Painting

Now about this painting. The secret for successfully painted animals, as well as for all clay things, is to see that there is strong dark tying them together and giving them accent.

Too, there should be a lot of one color and a little of the other. There should never be a 50-50 distribution. That would make for ordinary effect. Limiting the one color will make for distinction. Then don't put all the one color in one part and the other in another. Weave them in together.

Other than these general principles in the back of the teacher's mind, she need have no ideas. She should relax. The children will have lots of them.

Remember to say, every once in a while, "Paint it your own way. Don't worry how a cow really is." Children will do thrilling things. Direct, honest things, not the self-conscious, decorative effects of much modern adult pottery. Their sincere, naïve patterns remind us again of the wonderful power the child has in company with the primitive to use beautiful restraint unconsciously.

Now when we look at most children's clay work as it comes from the kiln we see that one big weakness is that the children have not put on enough layers of slip color. The coloring is streaked, washed-out looking. The white of the clay has come up to make itself known. So let us say now to our painters, "One more thing. Something you must never, never forget. One painting is not enough."

"I know. It's like a house. It gots to have two."

"Three," says another scornfully.

"You're both wrong," says the teacher. "Three is not enough."

Then Rudolph, wishfully imagining for himself a whole

day or two's painting, says, hopefully, "I think you paint him half a dozen times."

"Rudolph is right," says the teacher, while the children "Whew!" all about her. "Because what did we say about the clay itself?"

"It makes white color."

"If we put on just a little black or brick, what do you think will happen?"

"The white fight the black or brick, and win."

"It will look like dishwater—like in painting pictures, huh?"

"Yes, so we put on half a dozen coats to make a little blanket on top that we can see. If we let the colors run together any old way, we will just waste the precious color and have nothing worth sending anywhere. As our color gets too thick we will add more water."

So patiently, painstakingly, the teacher lays the foundation for the future.

This coloring process is tedious, but the children don't find it so. Here again keep your standard high. They can do it with care and genius. Have a little get-together period to check how well they have done it. If you think the cow has lost in the coloring, have the child go all over it again, clarifying, making greater interest. After firing will be too late.

Wasted Opportunity

Which reminds me that many teachers take the figures or bowls, or whatever the children make, unpainted to the kiln and call for the firing man to dip them in this colored glaze or that. They come out yellow or blue or whatever color asked for.

But I marvel at this as being the greatest wasted op-

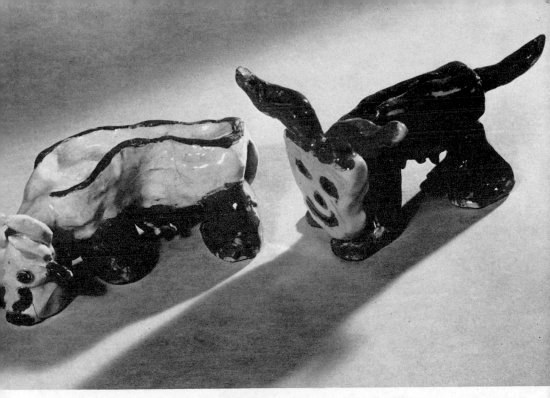

Why worry about how a cow really ought to be?

" closed my eyes and seen an angel and made one like I seen it."

The child will curve things unconsciously to fill his spac

portunity in the world. In the first place, whatever there was of child-like flavor in the shape itself is pretty well lost in this thick covering of colored glaze.   There is no chance for fine color, beautiful dark and light and the magic use of child's pattern.

Don't—don't do the one—the modeling process, without this latter that really makes for rich charm and personality.

It may be that some teachers have heard that clay colors are very expensive. Actually this is not so. This clay "slip color" can be bought at commercial firing studios for about 50¢ a pound. It is sold in as small as 5¢ and 10¢ packages. A quarter's worth of black and the same of burnt orange and brown will color, I should judge, twenty or thirty figures. Maybe more. There are many colors one can buy, but these, in combination with the white, will give a most satisfactory effect. Perhaps the teacher can requisition this "slip color" if she knows what to ask for. Or maybe her principal would give her a dollar from some fund, and dub it for school experimental activity. I promise the principal her money's worth many times over.

More Thrill than Christmas

The teacher will never have enjoyed Christmas more, even as a child, than the times when she calls for the children's box of fired things. Then is when she really learns too. She sorts over the fine from the ordinary, and tries her best to figure why. And oh, the thrill when she finds several that are truly distinctive!

If the first lot she has fired is not so good, she should ask herself:

Was the shape weak and uninteresting?

Was the color not strong enough?

Was the pattern without charm?

Above all, don't be discouraged. Consider this a challenge toward better effort in the future.

Just one final word. School has gone on while these children have been painting. Attention has been distracted. But think how much better your next clay lesson will go. Then too, nothing outstanding is ever accomplished without distraction and confusion anyway. You choose either the calm of the static regime or the general upset of creative adventure. It's the rare soul, if any, who can get both at the same time. Have confusion and don't care! You're working toward a program of growth and experiment.

The Master Cow-Maker

Make cows again the next time or two. Our main object, remember, is to free the child and give him confidence in his own way of doing. There is still plenty for the teacher to consider without jumping from one subject to another.

It is clear by now that Rudolph is our Master Cow-Maker. Who would have guessed that it would be he, shining like a star—the object of all our admiration? The children gather round him to exclaim. Always slow and embarrassed when confronted with written symbols, here he is as poised and sure as his Indian ancestor. Yes, I guess right. He says, "My grandmother makes deeshes in Mexico. She burns them in her yard."

Twice as many cows are saved this time. There is finer form—surer construction. Angela puts her cow down for an afternoon siesta, her legs and milk bag adjusted to her reclining position. Reminiscent of Ferdinand, someone puts a flower in his cow's mouth.

"Well now, we can't make cows all the time. How do we break away? Turn the children loose now?"

No, or you'll still get the all-too-familiar Mexican asleep under his great sombrero. Perhaps a little child will lead us.

La Madre de Guadalupe

Antonia says, "Why don't we make a Holy Mother, like down on Olvera? You know, La Madre de Guadalupe."

"Why not?" the teacher rushes to say, eager to grasp the opportunity to put to use the deep religious background of many of her children. The others have all seen the Madonna of Olvera Street, and enter into the idea with equal enthusiasm.

So we pass the clay.

"Splendid, Jesus! How beautiful, Alicia! How different everyone's in the room is. Nobody is worrying. Everybody is making it his own way."

"A long time ago we saw it in Olvera, huh?" says See Lee. "I didn't forget how it look. I keep it in my mind. Now when we make madonna, I take it out of my mind and put it in the clay."

"Yeah, I closed my eyes and seen an angel and made one like I seen it."

"I just love madonnas, the holy light around them and the way they gleam in the morning and evening. I just love to see them."

"I put the little round thing on top her head," says Rudolph, smashing a pancake halo into place.

"I put that veil that comes way down her. Christmas we dress Lucy for a madonna, huh? She look pretty because she got long braids."

"Sure, we put her on a chair on top of a table. We borrowed a real baby. It jumped up and down and chewed the pretty cloth and everybody laugh."

"In Mexico I think every house have a picture of the Holy Mother."

"Look, José says he don't want a baby. He puts in her hands a cross."

Lucille puts two little angels sitting atop her madonna's head. She says, "Why don't we make angels? Next time I'm going to make an angel with beautiful wings."

"Oh look! Maria has made her madonna with little bare feet! Look how cute they are."

"I do not make the Mother Mary," says Alicia. "This is the Guardian Angel, carrying to her the baby. See, I put the wings."

I look behind at the wings, and what is this I see? The guardian angel has great clawlike feet protruding from the rear. A remarkable expression of the primitive.

All over the room the creative spirit has taken hold. Someone makes a wayside shrine—a holy figure set in vaulted recess. Her right hand touches the forehead in the sign of the cross. Over the other arm hangs a rosary with crucifix.

A New Saint

Now what is this? All the children begin to shout, "Look at Trini! Look at Trini! Trini has himself in a coffin!" The teacher gasps. There he is, as though to revenge the world for finding itself at outs with him so often. An emaciated figure, ribs showing and loin cloth in place, inside a coffin, while on the lid, printed carefully, is the name of the owner, announcing from whose faithful form the spirit has taken wing.

We make madonnas again. The second time there are many angels and someone makes Jesus on the cross.

The third time there are many crucifixes. The angels and crucifixes, all strikingly different, are very near in pattern and feeling to the early Christian primitives that the art world treasures so highly. Beautiful things. Precious in their naïve sincerity. Strange, thrilling patterns, new to the world, save in those early days when men's hearts were as a little child's in approaching the Deity.

Every bit of effort we have put forth is now bringing return in enriched imagination and freedom and joy. There is a busy buzz in the room that comes only when the Master-Driver is at work—the Creative Urge.

From here, the children will have all sorts of ideas. But they won't be the Sleeping Mexican variety. Mother's Day brings mothers, arms encircling their children. And here is a figure of the teacher, done with such directness nobody could mistake. Figures of each other follow. Then figures of each other dancing.

"But how can we make Patsy her curls?" asks a non-adventurous one.

"Oh, that's easy," says Alicia, coiling tiny strings of clay around, ever so deftly.

We make horses, some with curls like Patsy's on mane and tail. But the outstanding feature of our making horses is—yes, you've guessed it—Hi-Yo Silver!

We made clay plates, but of those I will tell in the design chapter.

Congratulate Ourselves

How far we have progressed from those first cows that we thought so wonderful! No longer is anyone straining toward imitative adult perfection. We are drawing from the richer, rarer source of creative impetus.

Now we can trust a half-dozen to paint at one time. As this painting takes time, the children are let come in before school and at recess. We try to save for firing all the clay things that are truly beautiful. We put them on top of the cupboard till enough are ready for the firing kiln. Some schools have an arrangement for firing. Others are buying portable electric kilns. Otherwise clay things can be fired commercially for about 20¢ a piece. The idea is to have them so beautiful they will be worth many times the effort and expense.

"Pray to God"

Clay things, when dried, are very delicate, and horns and tails have a way of breaking off with scarcely any excuse. Time and patience should be left for getting them ready. They must be packed snugly, with plenty of wadded newspaper in between. The trip back, when they are fired, will be easy.

Then the teacher took our things to Lincoln High for Mr. Baddeley to fire them. I can just see her holding her breath as she went over the bumps. I bet she prayed to God to not have any of them broken, and none of them was.

Later they come back from the firing kiln as fascinating an array as anyone could wish for.

How glad we are that we persevered through the beginning stages till we reached this goal. And now an ever finer goal is before us, the child's creative genius leading, the teacher giving faith and understanding. A new and emotionally satisfying teaching technique is ours.

How infinitely worth while, helping the child to find inner harmony through new means of expression!

When I saw my clay things I was glad and happy. They look just like they came from a fairy book, they shine so and are so beautiful.

When the teacher brought back the clay things I was so anxious I just couldn't sit still. I felt some ants crawling about me, bees stinging me, and I was all jump.

Sometimes I go home about three o'clock and I have all my dress with clay and my mother say, "What do you got on your dress?" I say I was making clay in school. Then she tell me, "That's all right if you make pretty clay things."

Our teacher likes us to make clay things. Sometimes we make her tired, but then we make such interesting things her face smiles once more and I feel like dancing.

3. Design and Block Print

Design is the heart and soul of all children's craft work. Without design whatever they are making is ordinary, no matter how perfect the workmanship. With design it is a thing of rare charm and beauty.

The easiest way for the teacher to understand children's design is to think of their fascinating figures of people, animals, flowers, or other things woven together to fill space beautifully. As we give the child an appreciation for his own way of making things and something to make them on, he will pour them forth to fill space with rhythm and distinction. He does this not by thinking but by feeling.

When we look at children's design, we see more than childlike pattern. We see the design of primitive peoples through all the ages. We find the child making the same patterns that we find in museums of ancient art—even to the bearded cow.

First, as in everything else we undertake, we will take the child into our confidence: "In olden days people made everything they used beautiful, whether it was the handle of a knife or spear, pottery or woven thing. They put their heart and hand together to fashion it beautifully. This gave them a good feeling inside because they were expressing themselves, doing things their own way.

44

"Now people go to town to buy things and come back with their arms full, but inside they are empty—starved for the chance to make something beautiful. And the sad thing is, they don't even know what it is they are hungry for.

"Making things beautiful is called design. It is really just making pictures your own way and filling your space beautifully with them. It is easy for children to make beautiful design. Instead of worrying and trying to think things beautiful, you just feel them inside and they come out that way."

Paper Plates

The teacher will find that there is no more wonderful way to teach children's design than through the use of the rough, old-fashioned paper plate. She can stop in at any bakery and for a quarter carry away enough to give her children a rich design experience. Crayons and a can of shellac are the only other things needed to assure gifts as handsome as any mother's heart could wish.

So the teacher continues: "Today I have brought some paper plates for us to design. We will start with something that 'is our friend' as Albert says—a cow. Just as we have put our own pattern into clay, so will we put it on our plates. But first we will make sure that we are ready."

Our Own Pattern

"We will take our black crayon and make our cow pattern on our paper first. When it is interesting and strong and clear we will weave our red-brown crayon inside to make it more beautiful. Then we will swing our pattern around to fill the circle that we find traced on the other side of our paper. When we have done that beautifully, we are ready for a paper plate."

These first steps are easy for the children. All the teacher has to do is go up and down the aisles encouraging.

"Make it your own way—your own pattern."

"Swing it strong and clear."

The teacher must go about fighting "fuzziness." Over and over the first lesson or two the teacher must stress:

"Make your color velvet. Don't make it scratchy."

"My, what strong muscles John must have. His cow looks like part of the plate itself."

If a child makes a fussy attempt to copy a real cow, the teacher asks, "Would this make a beautiful plate, children? What kind of a cow do we want?"

"Our own pattern," they shout. "A design cow."

Children are wonderful. Even though the cow in the meadow may be all one color, it will come through the child's mind to form a clear-cut light and dark pattern. Where an adult would worry about how to put a straight cow on a round plate, the child will curve it unconsciously to fill his space.

The child will know how many cows to put in this circle. If he doesn't—he'll learn by trying. Often he will put two cows, their feet approaching in the middle of the circle —their backs curving near the edge of the plate. However, sometimes by making clever use of his space he will squeeze in three cows or even four, and still have them strong and beautiful. Or sometimes he will whirl just one cow around to fill his plate.

Edge Pattern

A band of color around the tiny flat edge of the plate and points shooting off from it at an angle around the slanting rim give light and dark to the rest of the plate. Flinging these rim patterns on at an angle gives movement. There is nothing static. They are alive and moving either with or against the cows.

The children will have as many different ways of making the rim pattern as they have the cows. Let us take just the swinging points for instance. They can shoot off from the edge of the plate long and at a great angle, or shorter and at a lesser angle. Or they can begin from the bottom of the slant rim and go up toward the edge. They can almost touch the edge or they can come far short of it. These points can be of one color or another or of the two adjoining. The band of color around the edge can be narrow or wide. It can be repeated in the groove where the bottom joins the slanting rim or it can be omitted entirely.

After a feeling for light and dark has been established through the use of these earth colors, many exciting things can be done with other colors. Painting the paper plate with water color first to give a background, and then using their crayons adds a new color experience. Continuing with the dark outline will insure depth and richness to these colors.

The children will do beautiful things. Just look to see that the same color is interwoven to tie the plate together and that there is quickness and life.

Dancing Plates

Next the children make "Ourselves Dancing" plates. Here again they work first for a jolly pattern, then swing it around a circle and then onto their paper plates.

They have painted themselves dancing and some of the children have made themselves dancing in clay. It is a simple matter to transfer what they have gained onto a plate. Indeed, the dancing itself helps here.

"You got to be a good dancer to design a good dancer," says one child, "Just like it said in a magazine, you got to be a good aviator to design a good airplane."

And so it seems. For the children are saying:

"See, I make her chest high and her shoulders down."

"I make her hair like a heavy train pull her."

"I make their fingers strong so the music can go out."

"I make them feeling the music down deep inside."

This last is Albert. I look long at Albert's. His great, awkward figures are bent forward, their backs pulling up, their heads and arms lowered in a feeling of inner repose. They have much the same feeling as the figures in Millet's "The Angelus," so familiar to the old-time schoolroom, but never seen by Albert.

"Beautiful, Albert!

"My, what fine plates! No paper doll patterns for the boys. Their patterns are their own honest way of making people.

"Good, Ignacia. You may skip the circle. Here's a real plate. I'm sure you can do it.

"Make your dancers as big and strong as your plate will let you.

"If you are making more than one dancer, keep your pattern the same. That gives us rhythm through repetition. Our eye likes to see the same pattern over again.

"See that all your lines are not the same width. That makes your design look ordinary. Widen some of your lines beautifully. Go over your pattern. Clean it up and make it velvet. You won't know how beautiful your plate is till you have done this.

"Beautiful, Willie!"

Willie has curved one jolly dancer around to make her

clumsy high shoes almost kick the jaunty bow on top of her head. Tiny little black button eyes are set close together, like a monkey's, and a great mouth is grinning delightedly from ear to ear. Arms are elongated, even as is the body, and swing down and up in a great arc to help fill the middle plate. Large, strong, uneven, rather sloppy points swing around the slanting rim of the plate to finish off the sauciest, goofiest, most charming dancer-plate that ever a non-reading, non-writing, non-figuring boy could make.

A tiny Chinese girl swings a chain of three stiff-legged dancers high around her plate. The arms start off from the bodies far down toward the waistline. Red-brown stripes on the dresses help the swing-around feeling.

Rudolph turns four identical profile figures around to make a wheel—their feet kicking toward the center of the plate—their heads going out into space, witchlike strands of gray-black hair trailing.

The legs of Manuel's dancers have the feeling of being encased in black, ribbed stockings as they are set wide apart near the opposite edges of the skirt.

Everywhere we find evidence of the child's own expression. One dancer, two dancers, three dancers, in every sort of organization. Some swinging around, some standing—all with life—their arms tossed out with abandon. There is a swagger pull to their figures, even though the legs in most cases are anchored firmly to the spot. Charming! No Hollywood here.

Here is no sterile copying or tracing or stenciling, but a live, breathing thing, giving the child creative joy and emotional satisfaction. We go over the same path we went with painting and clay. We find that nothing is lost. Our foundation is firm. We can build as we please.

Mounting the Plates

An effective way to display the plates is to slide two pieces of fresh tag-board together, top and bottom, or side to side, to get the proper size for the wall space, and pin them securely in place, and then pin the plates almost touching on top. Do not try to fill the tag-board, but leave a generous margin all around—a little more at bottom than top. Repeating this display in another available wall space more than doubles its thrilling effect.

Walter and His Plate

I have to laugh softly to myself every time I think of Walter, a new "problem boy" from Welfare, who came to our fourth grade late in the term. Shortly after his arrival the children began making plates.

"Good work, Walter," I said to him. "You have a real feeling for design. Now you may swing your cow pattern around your circle."

"Huh? You like that crazy stuff? That doesn't look like a cow. That's second-grade stuff."

"Ah yes, Walter," I said, "but there you are admitting it's good with your own words. Because, Walter, second-grade children know how to design and most big people don't."

"Humph! I still think it's no good. You like it—all right. I don't. See?"—said he, making a desperate attempt to cling to his idea of sanity in art.

However, Walter swung his cow pattern around his circle on the other side of his paper. There was a style and a rhythm about it. His design was good—there was no denying.

Not that I was wanting to deny it. I wanted desperately

to anchor Walter to something good that he could do, for he was in pretty bad shape inside. He was loud, insensitive. He would trip other people, rock his desk to make noise, make guttural sounds with his throat.

So I handed him a paper plate. He grabbed his crayon in show-off fashion, to have it all done in one minute. And he did. But it wasn't good. It had none of the merit of his pattern or circle design.

"Surely that's not what you've done with your paper plate? Do you think any old half-trying is good enough for us? Nobody wants a thing that isn't well done!"

"All right, you don't want it? Then I'll tear it up," he returned, grabbing at his plate.

"Oh no!" I went to battle with him. "Nobody tears up anything around here. You've wasted your plate and now you think you can act like a two-year-old and tear it up and that will make it right. Life will just give you a big boot if you act like that.

"I'm going to give you another plate. There's no hurry. You can spend all morning if you need to, but do a good job."

One could see that Walter was secretly liking the feeling that here was someone with authority. With a swaggering gesture, a bit less sure than before, he conceded, "Oh well, all right then, if that's what you want," and with a big-shot wave to the rest of the class, "if you like that second-grade stuff. . . ."

I could see that he was applying himself rather well. He can't work slowly, I decided. Too nervous. Cracking his knuckle joints in between times. In only a few minutes' time he had a design that was quite fresh and interesting.

"Shall I color the edge black and shoot some points coming down?" he asked, looking across the aisle with the corner of his eye.

"Sounds all right to me," I said. "It's all a matter of how you do them."

So he flung some black around the edge and red-brown points coming down weakly, headed any old direction.

I sauntered over and said, "What color is that around the rim?"

"Black. Don't you know black when you see it?" said he, extremely fresh. I refused to get excited. We were going to modify him not by repressing from the outside, but by changing him from within.

"Children, what color is this around the edge?"

"Dishwater," they all shouted together.

In a flash he went over his rim pattern, announcing that it was finished by tossing it high in the air and catching it on his head. I examined it at length and then ended my feud with: "Well, what did I tell you? You can do well if you try. Don't try to fool us any more. Put it up on the blackboard ledge, ready for shellacking."

Next morning I saw him out on the grounds, doing nothing in particular. So, wanting to clinch the gain I had made the day before, I sent for him. He came in, immediately on the defensive. "Well, what did I do? I didn't do nothing."

"Of course you didn't," I said agreeably. "But I thought you might like to make another plate. This time do it well from start to finish."

"Gee no! I want to play. School hasn't begun yet."

"Oh well, anyone can play. But not everyone can make an interesting design," said I impressively.

Our big thrill—making real plates.

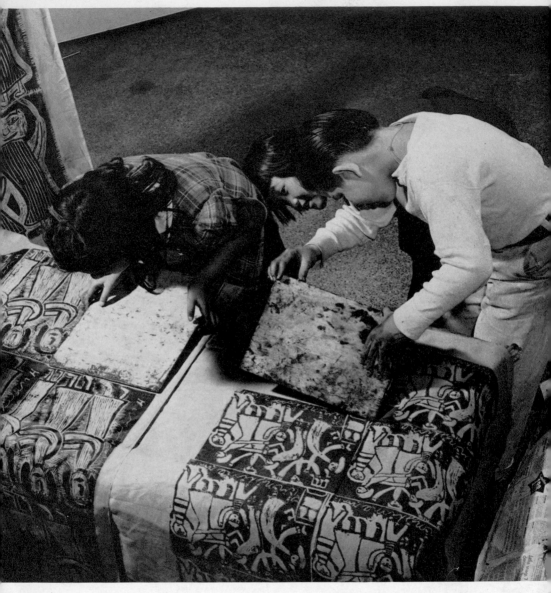

It is not the linoleum—it is the spiri

So with an elaborate show of regret, he sat down and started to work. I noticed he wasted less time in show-off business. He became absorbed. He continued even after the bell rang. He brought the plate to me with a quieter air than I had ever seen him have. I praised it and explained to the children that I had asked Walter to make another plate, as his had been really quite individual—quite distinctive the day before. I took his new plate and pinned it as part of our wall display.

When the recess bell rang, Walter waited to ask plaintively, "Can I go out and play?" Who knows, perhaps he was secretly hoping I would bulldoze him into more plate-making.

Of course Walter's plate, well done, was not just a plate. It was an entering wedge to get inside Walter and affect his feelings about himself and consequently the world in general. The plate was to help put his ego upon firmer ground so that the show-offishness, bumping, tripping, and bullying would be unnecessary.

Real Plates

Now for the big thrill, making real plates. It started under a little pressure, as most good things do. Our principal came in one day and said, "There's one thing I want you to do. I want you to make some real plates."

Then, being a good principal, she added, "I will make the molds and attend to the firing." So she brought the molds and we started in.

But first I shall tell how to make the molds. For since then I have made them many times and it is as easy as can be.

Making Molds

The first thing is to find a bowl large and shallow enough. A huge flower arrangement bowl is ideal.

Then stop in at a building supply house and buy forty or fifty cents worth of casting plaster. This should make six or more large molds.

When you have the bowl and the casting plaster, everything is easy.

1. Pour water into the bowl as deep as you want your mold. Two or three inches up the side will give your plate that lovely curve.

2. Then pour this water into whatever you are using to mix your plaster. It is the amount of water you need for the mixing.

3. Next, rub soapy hands over the inside of the bowl, removing any drops that collect. This will keep the mold from sticking.

4. Now shake plaster into the water till it begins to show all around on top like an island. Then you know you have put in the right amount of plaster.

5. Now put your hand in the mixture, pinch out the lumps and stir it about from underneath so as not to get it full of air. Stir it until your fingers begin to make tracks.

6. Then pour it immediately into your bowl, distributing it as evenly as possible. Then tap the sides to settle it.

7. You will notice that the mixture becomes quite hot after pouring. When it cools a bit, take the bowl very carefully to the sink and turn water over it inside and out.

8. Now turn it upside down and hit the sides. The mold will come out easily. If it doesn't, turn more water over it.

9. Now cut off a third of an inch around the edge so it won't chip.

10. Let it dry for a few days and it is ready.

While you're at it, make more molds. You'll want more than one so the children won't have to wait in between but can be making several plates at one time.

You will find these molds very precious. Other teachers will want to beg them from you. Just so does a little bother and work keep most people from doing things.

Making the Plates

Now needless to say, all your children won't be able to begin making plates at one time. Make one yourself first and then you will be better able to show them. Then choose a child that you have faith can do as you have shown. This child in turn can teach others.

First get a large old rolling pin and a piece of cloth, and see that the air is out of your clay. Then roll the clay to about half an inch thickness. Rolling it on the cloth makes the clay come off easily. Another piece of cloth on top keeps the rolling pin from sticking.

Now that the clay is rolled out, lay it over your mold, pressing it firmly all around. Don't be alarmed that it is half an inch thick. It will shrink in drying and again in firing.

The clay around the edge of the mold has a tendency to split, so tear a strip of cloth two or three inches wide, wet it, and drape it around the edge to keep the edge from drying more quickly than the rest of the plate.

When the plate has dried enough to hold its own, turn it over and lift out the mold. The casting plaster has sucked out the water from the clay so it will come loose easily.

Now trim the edges and the plate is ready.

This plate won't be perfect. It will be rough on the out-

side from the fingers pressing. It may be a trifle uneven here
and there. But who cares? Only machines can turn out perfect plates. And our plates will get better as time goes on. It
takes a little practice and experiment. And it is what we are
going to do to the plates later that really counts anyway.

Designing the Plates

We will go about designing the clay plates just as we did
the paper plates. Because the adjustment is great enough
without attempting untried patterns the child can take the
pattern with which he has already found success. Nothing is
more charming than a "cow" plate.

Designing clay plates is a rather difficult technique only
made possible by what has gone before. It can hardly become
an activity for all the children. For one thing the cost of
firing is too great.

At first begin with one child only. Choose a child who
has a strong feeling for design pattern and rhythmic space
filling.

For the first plate at least, have him swing his outline
pattern with black crayon on paper around a circle the size
of his clay plate. Then he can do the same with brush and
slip color upon his clay plate. The important thing is to see
that the design fills his plate beautifully.

Going inside this outline with burnt orange to greater or
less degree and finding some place for dark brown and yellow assures the plate a rich, beautiful coloring. By keeping
within the range of these earth colors at first the child cannot
go wrong. Also they are in keeping with the rough, hand-
hewn character of the plate. When other colors are used it is
well to dull them by adding a little black.

Although mistakes can be scraped off, such is not to be encouraged as it is apt to leave marks on the surface and tends to make the child careless.

After the pattern is swung around beautifully to fill the space, it must be gone over and over to assure rich, lovely color. The gum arabic we have added to the mixing water makes our job much easier. Ofttimes a swing pattern around the edge such as we used on our paper plates finishes the plate to advantage.

When the first child's plate is done, another child can be chosen to work with him. Soon a half dozen children can be designing at once.

Having the first plate or two fired as soon as possible will show how much of childlike feeling is being carried over and how well the colors are holding their own.

If the child has woven his own joyous pattern to fill the space with rhythm and abandon, the plate will have a rare charm and beauty that can be duplicated nowhere.

Now for Block Printing

"This morning I have brought something that isn't what it looks like at all. It is something tremendously exciting," says the teacher, unwrapping a bundle of scrap linoleum.

"I know—block prints!" shout some of the children.

"You make a picture and put it on the linoleum," says Jesus, struggling with the word. "Then you dig it out and put some ink and lift it up to make a picture."

"Fine!" says the teacher. "Come show how we do it!"

Jesus takes the new roller and dips it at the sealed can of ink, rolls it over a piece of linoleum, picks it up gingerly, and puts it on the cloth the teacher has spread for him.

"It gots to have something soft under," calls an initiated one. But despite the discrepancy, Jesus presses and pounds till the teacher suggests casually, "Why don't you stand on it?"

Hands begin waving. But Jesus hesitates only for an instant. Then he takes the chair Ernesto brings, with a bow and a flourish like part of a trapeze act, and climbs on the table. He steps onto the linoleum and teeters there, a bit wobbly as he tries to keep his feet from running over onto the cloth. This pleases the children immensely. He gets down and lifts the linoleum to see—nothing, of course!

But why waste your time in silly-business? Why not really get started? Because we are not wasting our time,—the children love silly-business,—and we are getting started. The children are gathering interest and catching enthusiasm. They can feel the rolling and tromping in their very bones.

The teacher explains about block printing. How it was done with wood, and still is, for that matter,—but now linoleum serves the purpose very well and is much easier.

The teacher says, "Children, linoleum won't make the block print, nor will the finest tools. What will?"

"Yourself! To make it your own way."

Then the children decide to take a theme they are all familiar with—themselves dancing.

"What must we do first?" asks the teacher.

"Make our pattern—make our picture!"

"Do not waste the precious space!"

"Make it swing to be jolly."

Block prints,—textiles capturing the child's own feeling, his own naïve expression! What could be more challenging, more exciting? If the teacher has never done block printing before, let her say to herself, "It is not the gouging, it is the feeling. It is not the linoleum—it is the spirit."

What to Do First

First we will make our design. The teacher passes Manila paper, size 9″ × 12″—the size of her pieces of linoleum. She shows the children how their paper will be the right size when they finish their design and lay it on the linoleum.

The children are eager. It is plain to see there are not as many pieces of linoleum as there are children.

They start outlining with crayons as they did in their plate design. They are filling their rectangle with dancing figures as they already have filled their circle space. There are as many ways of beginning as there are children in the room.

But what is Felicitas weaving all around her figures like great bands of spaghetti? The teacher waits to see and watches her add notes—quarter, eighth, and dotted whole. The G-clef comes in for more than its usual attention, being tossed here and there with reckless abandon as she "makes it swing to have rhythm." Tucked down in the corner is the small radio phonograph from which all the music flows.

Praise for All

As the teacher goes about encouraging, she sees promise of several block prints of distinction. When most of the children are done, she settles down to go over the designs with the children—evaluating—calling for suggestions. She finds some word of praise for all.

If one seems hopeless indeed, she can say, studying long and hard, "I can see where Manuel *almost* did something very interesting. He started, but then he grew afraid and tightened up and didn't let it come out. Manuel, if you had let yourself do that your own way, the way you felt it inside to do, you would have had something very interesting."

Poor, timid Manuel is pleased. He isn't quite sure about the good ideas he almost had, but then the teacher generally knows what she is talking about. And perhaps he *was* a little afraid and hadn't let himself go. He will try again to do better.

Tony's Design

As in the plates the boys made the most appealing figures. I remember Tony's design. His idea of jolly dancing figures seemed to be three doleful, hook-nosed figures trudging along as if going to a funeral. But the eye trained to respond to anything sincerely childlike could see that Tony's design was a prize. It had rhythm just as all sincere children's expression has rhythm. His figures pulled together as they trudged across the page. Not that Tony thought his figures doleful or lacking in any way. He showed no apology by word or look, nor did he need to. For Tony's design was beautiful—the beautiful that is not dependent on grace of form or feature. The world is so full of pretty pictures,—pretty design—growing more insipid with each look. Tony's design had character. It was one we would turn to look at again and again, trying to figure its peculiarly satisfying quality.

This Is It

But what of the block printing itself? This *is* the block printing, or about ninety per cent of it. The mechanics are nothing by comparison. If you have this childlike quality in the design, you can figure out the other for yourself, and with all your blundering still be miles ahead.

What We Shall Need

LINOLEUM. First we shall need linoleum, the brown inlaid kind—Battleship they call it. The thicker quality is best, but the thinner, softer kind will do for thin, shiny materials and is so much quicker.

When we get something very precious, we can go to a building materials place and they will cut us a thin piece of plywood to glue it onto, which relieves the wear of uneven pressure, and gives us a finer print, by the way.

TOOLS. Next we shall need block-printing tools. These are inexpensive and we can get along with three or four sets if we have to. Each set has an awl-like handle in which to slip the four or five tiny pen-point cutting tools that come in varying width and depth. The wide one that makes a shallow trench of almost a quarter of an inch is the one the children will clamor for. The tiny one is needed to go around the face pattern and other details.

BRAYER. Then we need an ink-roller or "brayer" to roll the ink onto the linoleum.

INK. And of course we shall need ink. School block-printing ink is printer's ink, which means it is black and thick like axle grease. It comes in pound cans and costs about fifty cents retail. Fine textile ink in various colors can be had, but costs three times as much or more. These textile inks will wash, so are much more desirable for anything fine.

TIN COOKIE SHEET. Then we must have something on which to roll the ink. A cookie sheet from the Five and Ten is just the thing.

PAD. The pad is important. We couldn't iron without a padded surface—no more can we block-print. A neat pile of newspapers with an old outing flannel blanket folded on top is ideal. We need the sponginess so the cloth will grip the ink and come up into the hollowed-out part of the linoleum to catch the tiny lines. A layer or two of old cloth will keep the ink from going through onto the pad.

CLOTH. For small children gold-colored cambric is very good, as the color is lovely and its shiny surface takes the print perfectly. Gold and yellow and orange sateen remnants are even more lovely. Wide, natural colored sateen remnants from the drapery department make beautiful, large-size prints for office or hallways. Wide margins top and sides and a little wider still at the bottom, frame the print to advantage.

CARBON PAPER. We shall need a few sheets of soft carbon paper to trace the design onto the linoleum.

ELECTRIC IRON. An iron is needed to iron out the wrinkles in the cloth as we go along. If we iron the cloth immediately before blocking each time, the heat will make the ink come off much better, giving us a finer, darker print.

Now, what else do we need?

Old rags, quantities of newspapers, and some cleaning solvent. You can guess what these are for. Block printing is a messy business.

Tracing with Carbon

After the design is done, the child traces it onto the linoleum. He spreads the carbon paper—two pieces—side by side if it is a big print—face down on the linoleum. Then he pins his design on top and traces over it very hard with a sharp pencil, being careful to remember every part. He must trace around the design outline outside and inside, following it perfectly in every little quirk. We don't want to lose one tiny bit of childlike flavor.

Going Over with Pencil

When this is done, he removes the carbon and design to see if his carbon outline has come through successfully onto the linoleum. Then he goes over this again with his pencil for fear the carbon will get rubbed off and lost.

Filling In with Crayon

Next he fills in the double outline with velvet black crayon. This should look now very much like the original. He should study it to see if it has the same form and feeling.

Later the teacher can save much time and effort by letting the children work directly on the linoleum with their black crayon widening and strengthening the lines as they did on their paper. A cloth with cleaning solvent or turpentine will remove anything unworthy.

Two Cautions

Now aside from two cautions the child is ready to go ahead.

The first caution is that every bit of this black crayon outline is to remain there. It is to be his design pattern which will show black on his block print. Suppose he lets his cutter slip? Maybe his dancer will lose an eye or a piece of arm. Black means Danger—stay away!

The second, and even more important caution is for the child not to let the cutter slip and bump into *him*. He must keep his left hand *behind* his cutter. That is one rule never to be forgotten. The cutter is sharp and with pressure behind,

can scoop into a hand just as easily as through harder linoleum. The child's natural inclination is to hold his hand opposite and in the direct path of his cutter. This he must
not do.

If the child obeys this one rule, no harm can come to him.

Cutting a Safety Ditch

Cutting a safety ditch around both the inside and outside
of all his black before he begins to gouge, is a good way to
protect it. In this way his cutter has no reason to come too
near.

Hollowing Out

Now that the black outline is protected by a tiny safety
ditch, the child begins hollowing out the inside spaces so the
ink roller cannot touch them when it passes over. This keeps
these parts white except for the edges of the scooped-out
places that may stick up to catch a little ink.

Sometimes when there are figures or things adjoining
each other, the child will go around the outside of each figure with little shooting lines. This gives a feeling of depth
and weaves things together.

Background

These same lines sent off from the outside of the figures
separate them from the background space without having to
hollow out all the background. It gives much the effect of a
halo going around the figures and is very beautiful.

However, the child will evolve his own way of handling
this gouging process. The most interesting things done will
be those inventions of the child mind that we can't even an-

ticipate. The imprint of the child's personality will be here as well as in his design. The slow, deliberate child will have a meticulously carved something, while the quick, high-strung child will show his inner restlessness in the imprint of every hasty, jerky move. We won't dig so deeply but what these tiny lines and crevices—this design within a de-sign—will show.

Printing

Imagine the excitement of the owner when his block is "feenished." The excitement is catching. Everyone in the room is eager for the initial printing. We might as well stop everything and gather around. Jesus opens the can of ink, and puts a tablespoonful on the cookie tin. Then he dips into a little bit of the ink and rolls until the ink is spread evenly over his brayer.

The brayer should have plenty of ink but not in tiny gobs, or they will get into the crevices. These in turn will make sticky places on the print. A little experimenting will teach the child when he has enough ink to get a fine, dark print and yet not have it too black and tarry looking.

Putting Pressure

Inking the block properly is only half the job, remember. There must be pressure applied after it is laid on the cloth. If the block is small, our electric iron helps.

Now the children are making larger blocks so Jesus puts his pad down on the floor where he can stand on it.

It takes clean hands to keep the unprinted part of the cloth pulled up to the center of the pad. It takes clean hands for hanging it on the wall to dry. So Jesus, his blackened hands showing the world who is in authority, relegates tasks to others.

Now I can't conceive of a whole roomful of children all block-printing at the same time. No one teacher could supervise it for one reason. And where would they get the tools and materials for another? Half a dozen block prints being worked on while the class is doing other things keep a teacher pretty busy.

I remember the quick, charming design Ignacia made. But she showed no interest in executing it. She was afraid protracted gouging would take too much time from reading her library books. So we let José do it for her. He dug contentedly off and on for a week. Others helped with the printing. Still others cleaned the block and tools afterward.

Care of Materials

That brings me to care of materials. When the children have made these blocks spilling over with the charm of their own expression, have them take good care of them. Let the children go over the blocks with cleaning solvent, removing all the sticky ink. Otherwise the tiny lines and sharp-cut features will become dulled by many coats of hardened ink. Have them take good care of the tools that will help make more such blocks. Let them go over the roller with solvent and all in and around the handle. They will need it to spin around well next time. Have them press the heavy waxed paper down snugly over the remainder of the ink in the can before putting the lid on tightly or the ink may be all granulated when they open it again. Have them scrub the table, and themselves. They will need it.

Be encouraged that from one beautiful block can come any number of prints.

Follow Child's Interest

Subjects for block printing follow the children's own interest. After "Ourselves Dancing" we made "Ourselves Block-printing." Several of their designs were good, with printer and others gathered around the table on which one could see roller and linoleum block and print already made. However, for most of the children this was too difficult. As a general rule block prints should be less complicated.

For instance, when the children painted the school cafeteria they put the line of children, the stoves, the refrigerators, the electric fan, the helpers, and the steam tables. This would be too confusing for a block print. So we would narrow the subject down to perhaps the one, saucy, tilted figure of Mrs. Johnson lifting high the steaming kettle or pulling out the apple pie in front of the great, hooded stove. That much would give the feeling more than if we tried to show the whole setting.

The Maypole, with its rhythmic pattern of children flinging through space with upraised arms holding the ropes, makes a perfect subject. We can take a hint from Jesus and put the circle that feet have worn in the earth underneath.

The children's animal patterns can be carried over almost directly from their plates. Why not make a block 11″ by 13″, or even larger, with animals—two together, with feet approaching, to fill the rectangular shape? Great, beautiful, rhythmic horses, let us say, with faces the way the child thinks they look—with manes the way the child thinks they grow. What a beautiful, thrilling thing this could be!

In Conclusion

Children love block-printing. They love the tarry smell of the sticky ink. They love the rolling and the pressing. The cutting satisfies like whittling on the old-time school desk. And even the teacher cannot fail to be drawn by the element of chance that plays a large part in the best block-printing and causes her to bate her breath while the block is lifted.

Block prints have been made for centuries, but the most beautiful thing remains largely undone—that is, to catch the charm of children's own naïve expression.

The best of luck to you!

Block prints—textiles capturing the child's own feeling.

"Don't worry how others are doing it.

4. Free Rhythmic Dancing

This dancing, like children's art, is not dependent on background. In fact, as in their art, it can be a good thing if the teacher is unencumbered with old ideas on the subject.

What the teacher needs is faith and understanding. Faith that there is the capacity within the child to do surprisingly beautiful things when encouraged and freed by the teacher—understanding that children's dancing is not a thing of steps, of artificial movements to be learned by rote.

The moment we concern a child with steps, we tie him up, inhibit his free movement, make him fearful, put false emphasis. The walk is ruined if we ask the child which foot he puts forward first. He just naturally walks following a desire within him. So also will the child dance.

"You say the teacher doesn't teach the child steps—doesn't tell him what to do? Well then, what does the teacher do?"

The beautiful dancing is in the child already. What the teacher does is to remove fear and embarrassment and help it come out.

Joy Comes from Within

We like to believe that all children are happy within themselves—free to act joyously. Such is wishful thinking. For years the child has been taking on the tensions of the family, the schoolroom, of life all about him.

We are not even right in believing the very young child to be free. I have watched Miss Gertrude Copley take little three-year-olds. Many of them would come to her tense, constricted like little old men and women. Only by her gentle understanding and calm assurance could they open up to give out the response to rhythm that is inherent in every child.

We cannot free the child with outer imposed rhythm. We cannot argue, "The Swedish people danced this with joy and abandon. Therefore this will contribute to the child joy and abandon."

Joy and abandon are only gained through working from within. It is the emotions that control the deep muscles inside us that govern our breath and being. The child's body is free only when we have set it free through giving faith and confidence to the child emotionally.

Is the Teacher Ready?

But first, is the teacher herself ready emotionally? Has she cast out all feelings of failure based on past dancing experiences? She must be without fear and tension. She must believe that it can be done.

I remember teaching my first year in a small town where there was very little to do, so I sought out a dancing class. There we limbered ourselves on side-bar contraptions, "stretching exercises" I believe they called them. I was most respectful. I challenged none of it.

We had a recital in the town's biggest theater. We adults were to dance to the Egyptian Ballet music from Aida. I had taken several private lessons to help bring me up to the level of the group. On the strength of these the teacher put me at the head of the left-hand procession. She made a big mistake.

She wasn't counting on the emotional angle which I am stressing to you as so all important.

The nervousness of the occasion, coupled with my own well-seated unbelief in myself in general and in dancing in particular made the results of my private lessons vanish on the spot. The music began. I held up the whole line before I could get started with the left foot, right foot business, whatever it was.

I had needed the private lessons, but more than that I had needed going over emotionally, so that I could have found confidence and faith.

That experience left its scar, I can assure you. I winced for years whenever I heard that same music. Very likely failures in years since have had their inception in the bungling of affairs that night.

Perhaps you have had other experiences of a lesser nature. Maybe as a child they stressed the fact that your sister was so graceful, allowing you to gather that that quality was not yours. Or as a teacher you have found yourself unable to master a supposedly simple folk dance that you have been teaching off and on for many seasons. Perhaps you wonder what is wrong that you persist in forgetting which arm the children are supposed to curl in under.

Fine! Don't be discouraged and think, "Dancing is not my forte. I have no gift for such." The very fact that you haven't found yourself in rote rhythm work may very well mean that you are the type that needs something other to call forth your best interest and effort. You were not at fault—the dance was.

But before we begin we will take the children into our confidence somewhat as follows:

"There are many kinds of dancing, but the most beautiful

dancing of all is that dancing which is inside us already—that we don't have to go anywhere to take lessons to learn. We don't have to have ever danced before in our lives. All we have to do is to let it come out of us. It comes out as we feel the music."

Then we will start freeing the child emotionally as we present step by step the simple, easy fundamentals of this dancing.

Moving from a Body Center

The most important underlying thing about this dancing that the teacher will learn to present and to watch for is the moving from our diaphragm or body center. This body center is alive, expanding, contracting with everything we do. Moving from this body center gives us beautiful co-ordinated movement. In everything we present to the children we will be working toward this end.

Bouncing in a Circle

The first thing we will have the children do is to waken and expand their body center through bouncing in a circle. We say to the children, "It's just as though we have a ball inside us here," pointing to our diaphragm. "It bounces and the rest of us has to bounce with it. We feel it bouncing in our tummy. It bounces in our fingertips. It bounces all through us."

We play "Pop Goes the Weasel" or any jolly folk dance record and the children bounce up and down with the music.

We explain to the children that we are like a puppet held high by a string, our legs dangling. The string holds us up where we can bounce beautifully.

We praise and encourage with everything in us, giving

the children confidence. Taking the girls first and then the boys makes for less embarrassment at the beginning. Such dividing will cease when there is no longer any need of it.

Although delicacy and sensitivity play a great part in this dancing, the strength and power can be emphasized for the boys at the beginning. They have so much heritage of "sissy-talk" to overcome.

This bouncing idea is not difficult. The teacher will begin to see how raising and expanding the body center gives life to every part of us. It lifts us up above the hips where we can move freely. It is as though the body were suspended from the air rather than propped up from the floor. Our shoulders can relax and drop softly into place. Our head is in line to push high in the air. Pressure is removed so we can breathe more freely.

Truly this body center idea is working wonders already.

Now the Rock

"Yes, the bouncing idea is easy enough to get, but what comes next?"

Something just as easy.

We're going to rock back and forth in the circle. We will go from the heel of our foot up onto our toes with a simple, rocking movement.

"It's like pumping high in a swing," we tell the children. "We couldn't get very far if we just moved our arms back and forth like spaghetti. It is the big push up we give with our center that makes us go high."

So we work patiently in a circle, first girls and then boys. Holding hands in the circle gives the child a feeling of security. He is assured of not being stranded out on his own.

Practise this. Suppose you don't get it exactly as it is suggested here. What harm is done? The important thing is for there to be a lift inside which brings the whole body into line.

And with the music we chant slowly, "Rock up" with the first part of the music, and "Then we come down" with the answering music.

"Chinese Lullaby" (Victor Record No. 21970A) is good for this because the music is so clearly divided for the upswing and the down.

A Positive Thing

"But suppose," you say, "there are some children who refuse to come when beckoned? What shall we do?"

Well, every group is different. But in the first place, try to feel it down deep inside you that everyone will come. Have your voice relaxed and casual, suggesting successful response. Then a kindly word or two, "Yes, we're all going to come to the circle. Come Helen. Come Cruz. We are waiting for you."

If there is a child who just will not respond and who is miserable at the thought, don't press him. This dancing is going to be a positive thing, born of praise and happy association. Human nature being such as it is, he will want to share your approbation. He is trying you out—watching with all eyes to see what happens when a child doesn't know how. When he sees there is no singling out of the individual for censure for his shortcomings, but only praise for the thing well done, he will lose his fear and nine times out of ten, be ready to go forward in a day or two. Don't let him sit there day after day without gentle urging, however. The first few days are crucial—to go or not to go. Summon patience and wisdom to get up all possible.

"Sissy—Sissy"

I remember a bright little Chinese boy, who came to our fourth grade direct from China. He was very sensitive and easily embarrassed. His whole background seemed to suggest that such wasn't the thing for boys to do—in China at least. Although he knew little or no English, it didn't take him long to learn to say, "Sissy, sissy," in self-defense at the boys dancing. I soon felt the odds were too much against me and gave up pressing him.

During the whole year and a half he was with us, never once did he dance. Then the last week or two his friends got him up, took him by the hands, patted him on the back, made a great to-do about his coming, for they were very fond of him. Naturally he was embarrassed, but very proud and happy to have gathered the bravery to do as the others did at last.

The time was over before he fairly got started. It has troubled me ever since that I did not find a way somehow to get him out of his seat sooner. I had accepted defeat until it was too late. He, the one child who had needed it above all others I was content to pass over, supposing it to be the impossible.

Maybe he could have danced some of the soreness out of his poor little self, so he would have been saved the big trouble he got into by learning to say "Japanese pipple no good. Japanese pipple bah!" and tormenting our timid little Yoshiko.

The Fold

But now to go back to the Rock. The Rock is really only the forward movement in which we push up with our center.

The backward downward movement we will call a Fold. In it we let our body softly drop.

We are like an accordion opening and closing. We open as we rock up and close as we fold back. This gives our movement contrast.

Next let us widen the circle and try running a little forward as we rock up and a little backward as we fold down. Already we have something beautiful.

Hands and Arms

The part the arms and hands play in this dancing is very simple. They do nothing to call attention to themselves as appendages. They are part of the inner movement itself. We might say they are like the great branches of a tree moving only as the trunk moves.

In the old dancing there was an elaborate technique for the arms and hands because there was little else happening.

Because the arms and hands move from within at the center, they have a beautiful feeling of weight. The movement of the one arm or hand is reflected in the other. It is the same feeling as though we have great elastic bands around both hands that have to be pushed back as our hands move apart and away from each other.

We can help the children to get this feeling of weight by having them bring up sand on the palms of their hands. "Up with hands heavy—and down," we say in tempo with the music. The children's faces are seriously intent as all eyes follow the hands strongly raising and lowering with their imaginary burden.

"Always when we move our arms and hands we feel them *squdging* in our center.

"A little hollow space under the arms helps keep our

body poised and free. Squashing our arms down means our shoulders are hunched."

We show the children how to send something alive from our center way out through our finger tips.

"We feel our fingers alive when we dance. We send out the music from them. Weak, curled-up fingers are dead," we say.

And over and over again we say to the children as they dance, "Strong hands are beautiful."

Legs and Feet

Our legs and feet also move from our center. When we take a step we put our foot down right out of our center. This gives our step weight. But it is a beautiful, vibrant weight, not the heavy trudge from the hip.

"Our foot is not like a stick of wood," we tell the children. "It has the same parts as our hand, only our toes are the fingers.

"We feel our whole foot like the Indian does. It is just like stepping in the mud. We get that same *squdgy* feeling."

Then we take a moment to feel.

"Heel—palm—toes—*squdge*!

Heel—palm—toes—*squdge*!"

We can practise raising sand on our toes, as we did on our hands, lowering it carefully so it won't spill.

"Now we are getting something beautiful in our legs and feet."

Our Neck

Our neck also starts moving not at our shoulders, but from deep down within at our body center. This gives our head the feeling as if we have a tall, Spanish comb upon it that reaches nearly to the ceiling. Moving our neck from within gives it weight and meaning.

We Suggest a Turn

From here we continue, making the children more and more independent. We suggest a turn as they go forward, scooping the heavy air, and a turn again as they fold backward. This is suggested casually, as though it were as easy as breathing. "Just tuck in a little at your center and scoop around." If there is a child hesitating to know how to make this turn, say to everyone, "Just make it your own way. Don't worry how others are doing it."

Soon the children will be making independent turns. "That was a fine turn," we say to the timid one. Then we can explain, "A little bigger tuck tilts the body to one side beautifully, our center rising high on the upswing. Beautiful José! Watch how he turns it from his center, his hands strong, scooping the air."

The children are still in the circle. There is safety, emotionally, in numbers. The teacher avoids seeming to gaze hard at the timid ones. She praises, poor dear, until she feels quite exhausted. She must not hurry this beginning phase. It is the important one. Casting the children out upon their own before they are ready is like throwing a child into the water to teach him to swim. It may leave emotional scars that will take a long time healing. Better go too slowly than too fast.

Forget the Circle

Then comes the pertinent step—the major operation. Keep this forward and turning and backward and turning in the circle till you feel sure the children are ready. Then say, "It's too bad we don't have more room to do it beauti-fully. Maybe . . . do you suppose we could forget the circle and just turn it anywhere? Turn it all around the room. Fill all the space. Ready—turn everybody. Beautiful, Helen! Beautiful, Maria! It is so much easier with more room to do it. Just keep the string pulled high and do it your own way. Now let us try the boys—" or girls, or however you are dividing them.

And the children go moving about sincerely, turning as they feel the music.

Now we are making a big gain because we are divorcing the children from the security of the circle. Through praise and encouragement we are doing this. But this is a very delicate step. Feel those children whom fear is already start-ing to take hold of again, and work fast and hard that they shall gain confidence—feel successful.

Now! This was the hardest work we will ever have to do. In fact, this beginning phase is the only hard work we will have to do. Later, and I speak the truth, the teacher's role is to sit at the back and enjoy what the children bring forth —her only responsibility, an easy one, to give praise when she sees something beautiful.

This first *is* hard work, but it is infinitely worth while and will bear fruit abundant. It is hard work because we are dealing not with the body, but with the emotions. The wall we are breaking down is one of self-consciousness and em-barrassment the child has been building since he was an infant.

If you have the children out of their seats, you have done wonderfully. If you have them raising and expanding their body center and beginning to move from this point, they are well along the way. If you feel muddled inside, you have a right to feel so. Remember this is the first time you are working this through. Congratulate yourself if you have only partial success.

Into the Future

Now let us stop for a little inspiration. Let us go forward into the future, to a room program. The children are barefoot and dressed for the occasion. The girls have on simple costumes they have made from unbleached muslin dyed various shades of gold and henna and mixtures of the two. The boys have on men's shirts dyed the same beautiful colors. The bottoms of the shirts are pulled far out to make a great blouse. The long sleeves are fastened tight at the wrists with rubber bands so they can blouse also. The collar with its band is turned under. No amount of sewing could make anything so attractive. The warm colors bring out the rich, dark coloring of the children.

An inexpensive electric box phonograph is on a table at one side of the room. The teacher calls to Ernesto to put on Liszt's "Hungarian Rhapsody No. 2, Part I" (Victor Record No. 14422 A). The children sit up eagerly. It is their favorite music. The teacher waits till there is an absolute hush, and then nods to the phonograph caretaker. The stirring first notes of the "Rhapsody" begin. Eyes are begging, pleading that their owner be called to start the dance.

"Dolores May Take It"

The teacher says from her comfortable perch at the back of the room, "Dolores Garcia may take it." Dolores Garcia starts from her seat, already having captured the spirit of the music. Hers is the slow, strong movement that begins at the very center of her being and pulls from her toes way out through the tips of her strong fingers. Beautifully sincere, absolutely without self-consciousness she moves, feeling the music from down deep inside her. Her arms are moving, yet one is not conscious of arms moving because it is her whole body moving, moving from within.

"Boys May Go"

Now the first part of the music is ending. A dynamic second part, ideal for leaps and jumps, is about to begin. Already boys are half turned in their seats, ready, eager for their cue.

"Boys may go," the teacher says calmly, and beginning where they are, in the various parts of the room, boys move in tempo with the music, anxious to get to the front of the room before the music gives its first great leap.

Then there begins as beautiful a sight as one could want to see. Twelve or fifteen boys, unconscious of all save the joy that is in them, dancing this second part of the music, following the music, catching one great jump after another, just as plainly as if the music were really crying out "Jump—jump" at intervals, and most remarkable of all, seldom, if ever, bumping into each other.

"All Right—Everyone"

Now there approaches a third part of the "Rhapsody," a slow, waltzlike movement which seems to promise that many children could dance without interfering too much with one another. So before the last jump is ended, the teacher calls, "All right, everyone!" and then commences a thrilling exodus forward, in which nearly every child, upon the word, leaves his seat, already carrying the mood of the music, and goes forward to join the great mass movement—the expression of every moving, weaving body absolutely sincere, honest, without self-consciousness or affectation.

Then follows a joggety movement in which we hear the children's bare feet thumping on the floor. And then, what is this? Almost everyone upon hearing a quick little whirring music corkscrews his body from within and whirls with the music. Beautiful!

The music changes back to the waltzlike part and the children catch it on the instant. As this next part of the music nears an end, the teacher calls "Everyone come back, leaving Alice, Dolores Garcia, John, Joe Ling, Eileen, Raymond, and Armando. Bring the music back with you to your seat. Don't drop it off. Lovely, Antonia! Beautiful, Joe Salvadore!"

The music gives a great lurch forward and begins to die down. Bodies are suspended in air, motionless save for a little pulsing beat in time to the almost inaudible accompaniment, awaiting what is to follow. But what are some of the children doing? They are dropping down sitting up, you might say. The string is still pulling their centers high, but their knees have softened, letting the body ooze down toward the floor. Several are turning as they lower, arms balancing at the sides. There is that feeling within them of the music dying down, absolute quiet, save for that tiny inner pulsation. But now! The music is beginning to grow and swell. Their bodies are rising, turning from within as they shoot upward into space.

They go off into the last part of the music which is a repetition of the first, while the teacher calls "Everybody may finish with them," and the seats empty again in a beautiful surge forward, to create something beautiful, individually and as a part of the whole.

"Bring Back the Echo"

The record ends and the teacher says, "Don't drop the music. Hold it to the last. Then bring the echo beautifully to your seats. The children file silently back, while a visitor confides, "It brought tears to my eyes, it was so beautiful." They are quiet for only a moment, until someone begs softly, "Again. Let us dance it again—please!"

"Very well," someone says. "No doubt this free, spontaneous dancing is sincerely beautiful. But doesn't your very description belie your assurances of the first part of the chapter? It is full of 'first part of the music,—second part,' etc. The teacher must have background, must know music—must be able to analyze it into its parts."

No, it does nothing of the sort. The only knowledge the teacher has of the divisions of this music is what she has felt without intellectualizing, while watching the children dance it.

Feeling the Music

But let us go back. Let us see how we got this far. We left off with our hardest work over—our foundation laid. The children were turning freely about the room—"filling all the space."

Now we come to the most significant phase of all—the sincerity with which the children feel the music. This is what will strike everyone who sees your dancing. There is no staginess, no affectation, no artificiality. We do not mention this outside to the children. It comes from stressing the feeling tone inside.

We begin by saying, "You know already, children, that it is not how we move on the outside that counts, but how we move from the inside. Also it is how much we *feel* on the inside that counts. It is better that we stand still and feel the music than move about without feeling anything. When we stand still, our bodies, our faces will be beautiful because we are feeling something beautiful deep inside. When we move about and do things without feeling it is just like something empty rattling.

"And when we feel the music, it will come out our own way. It will be different from anything anyone else is doing. It is bound to be. Just as our painting is different. Just as we ourselves are different.

"So never worry how someone else is doing it. We don't want you to do it that way. We want it your own way— your own pattern. The music will tell you what to do."

"But are children capable of responding to the music, as you suggest? After all, aren't most of them rather insensitive to such?"

By no means. Children are far more susceptible to beauty than adults. They haven't had time for the divine spark to be extinguished.

We can test this beautiful feeling as well as we can test arithmetic. Better and more surely.

Let us put on "In a Monastery Garden" (Victor Record No. 35808) and say to the children somewhat as follows. "Now we are going to find those people who can feel the music down deep inside. This piece is called 'In a Monastery Garden.' It has the same feeling of quiet and peacefulness that we feel in a church. In fact, it is a church piece, for a monastery, you know, is a place where the monks, or holy fathers, live their whole lives in study and prayer. The only sound you will hear, besides their singing, is the tolling of church bells. Let us see if we can feel that beautiful peace

"It is how much we feel on the inside that counts."

Ever-increasing variety of movemer

inside us. Before you start from your seats, take time to feel the music. If you don't, that part is just wasted."

In this "Monastery Garden," or "Ave Maria" (Victor Record No. 7103) the whole record is in this same feeling tone, so the teacher and children can concentrate on this one mood.

The teacher calls the name of her strongest dancer, saying, in tempo with the music, "Feel it down deep inside, Dolores, to make it beautiful. How beautifully Dolores feels the music. She feels it deep down inside. It shows on her face, her neck, every inch of her body. See how she plays all the notes with every part of her. I wonder who will be next to feel the music. Joe Salvadore try it. Very beautiful. No, don't lose it, Joe. Go right on feeling it down deep inside. Armando and Raymond try. Very beautiful indeed. We can fool no one. They will know if we are thinking of ourselves and those watching, instead of feeling the music.

Teacher Must Care

"Thank you. That was very beautiful. Now everybody try."

Think back to your own childhood. You would have tried to get a similar appreciation from the teacher.

All this, of course, must be done with sincerity on the part of the teacher. If the teacher doesn't really care and is only half-hearted, she will get little worth caring about and only a half-hearted response.

If you are lucky enough to catch a child in a sincere moment who usually makes a point of scoffing at dancing as sissy, capitalize on it. Say, "How very beautifully José was feeling the music a moment ago. Just for a moment—but it was there. If we have felt deeply like that once, it will come again easily. We can never lose it."

Maybe José is now bumping at everyone he can. That's fine, your words have struck their mark. He is admitting it as much as any he-boy can by trying to cover his feelings in embarrassed silly-business.

Which brings me to silly-business. Silly-business is all right. In fact, I believe it is necessary. It is a random movement that will be dropped off as you go along. Have the door closed and relax. If someone makes a big show of falling on the floor, stay relaxed. Don't tighten up. The floor can take it. After he has fallen on the floor once or twice, the novelty will be over.

Try never to say the negative word in this dancing. Remember again that very likely the one who is annoying is really the one who is caring most about it, but has to go through a show of not caring to prove he is not a sissy.

When a child is giggling and bumping into others, it is a sure give-away that he is not free of embarrassment, but is trying to cover his inner feelings by these outer overt actions. They are symptoms that all is not right as yet within.

Of course if someone just fails to respond and makes himself too much of a nuisance, we can say very casually, "Oh Albert, come on back. You're just being silly. You're not ready to dance yet." But don't let us put an edge to our voice. Remember we're going to see these first few weeks through to something fine and beautiful. We can't afford to let anything annoy us.

If we continue positive—just praising the good and ignoring the evil, he will surprise us by falling in line. As sincere effort and expression receive the recognition and praise, there will be no object in continuing the other.

Just as we can dig a channel to control the direction of a stream, we can control the direction of our children's activities through praise and recognition.

"Music Won't Let Us Bump"

If there is too much bumping we can say, "If we bump, we are not feeling the music, because the music won't let us bump. Just try very hard and see. The music makes us feel in the air just who is near us, so we can slow down and go in between."

There is much truth to this, because the child who is embarrassed and thinking of himself is usually the one who is bumping here and there. As he loses his embarrassment, his attention goes instinctively toward better guiding of himself among the others.

"The music gives you eyes in the back of your head," the teacher says.

"You have to watch where you're going," says Roberto. "Don't just bump people like a drunk man. Don't laugh and everything when you dance. That means that you're ashamed. Don't be ashamed. It's nothing to be ashamed of."

"Funny Dance"

I remember a boy named Howard who came to our room. He had been pulled out of Main Street movies during school time. It is his Circus Story you will find on page 115. We noticed in his dancing that he had wonderful rhythm but preferred to act silly mimicking and acting the fool. So we asked him to dance for us.

"Dance funny," the children begged all over the room. The boy was clever! He showed real talent. Soon a funny little American boy who had been adopted and raised in

Mexico and couldn't speak English beckoned if he, too, could go.

Together they went through antics as well as if they had been a well-rehearsed vaudeville team. Of course one had to loosen up and put himself into the spirit of the occasion. While one looked the other way, the other kicked him in the pants and then glided innocently off to pluck a flower from the desk and dance, gazing at it in the most aesthetic fashion.

Through some kind of intuitive agreement they came forward as a singing duo. One started out trustfully in an affected falsetto voice, only to have the other fail to accompany him. Then the first mix-up over, he started again in seeming faith, only to have such happen again. The children loved it. There was time off to get tuned up with important clearings of the throat and voices jumping unexpectedly into squeaks. Then one directed the other with great flourishing movements and long-held notes. They patted each other on the cheek. Then they danced again, finally the one stooping over for the other to ride on his neck. Out one door they went, and in the other, with elaborate bows from the one on top, to the delighted audience.

"Why did you tolerate such?" Ah—I had my good reasons. In the first place, these boys had a gift for this type of thing. Everyone should have a chance to express and develop himself according to his gifts. Actually this is a rather rare and highly compensated commodity. No doubt there are those in Hollywood not half so gifted making many times the board superintendent's salary.

But the real reason we had these two boys clown was that they had it in their systems and were using it in negative fashion to bother and disrupt. It was an unspoken agreement that in exchange for the one they dispensed with the other. Or maybe it was just that they got the other out of their systems or found it unnecessary now that they were being recognized as popular members of the group.

We had some company one day and we thought we could risk having the "Funny Dance." I guess it was too much to expect. One visitor said to my principal very seriously, "I sat wondering what the boys were trying to express." The principal said she thought quickly, groped for some educational principle in my defense, and then told them, "Well, you know they say we are supposed to start with the children right where we find them, and that was undeniably where she found them."

Joyous Expression

But to get back. We left off testing the children for quiet feeling tone with the beautiful "Monastery Garden." Now let us give the same attention to the joyous mood. Here we have a dynamic "throw away" type of movement. Play "Grasshopper Dance" (Decca Record No. 495) or any jolly folk dance for joyous abandon, praising all the while. "My how gloriously free and happy Eileen dances this. Watch what a lot of space she covers. The music is just bouncing all through her—through her toes up to her finger tips. Watch her skip and turn. See how she throws the music out—throws it big and free from her center. She just seems to be part of the music itself.

"Now everyone may dance. Dance it your own way! Make your own pattern!"

Nearly every piece will have these two moods in combination. I hesitate to suggest definite records. The teacher should choose the music that she is happiest with. However,

I find in getting started at least, a gypsy type of thing, such as "Dark Eyes" (Victor Record No. 20037) with "Two Guitars" on the back, is very fine. These go from the sombre sadness of the gypsies to the joyous abandon of their more happy, carefree moods. The changes are clearly marked. "Persian Market" (Victor Record 35777) with "In a Chinese Temple Garden" on the back are both pieces the children love. Brahms' Hungarian Dances can follow later.

Now is your big thrill. As we saw in the "Hungarian Rhapsody," the children will switch from the one mood to the other without a moment's hesitation. You don't have to call their attention to it one single little bit. You don't have to point out and analyze the changes. You don't have to be able to anticipate what the children should do. They will make these changes without coaching—without guidance or help on your part. If a child wants to run at play, he can do so. You don't have to tell him how. If he wants to go slowly, thoughtfully, he will go so. He can do the same with the music. When it changes like a flash from the sombre to the brilliant, he will change, because the music makes him want to. A few words of praise is all that is needed.

"My, how beautifully John caught that change in feeling. How wonderfully Angela caught it too. You all did very well indeed."

So praising—praising—praising, we grow.

Jumps

It will not be long before you will see someone—most likely a boy—attempting some kind of jump for emphasis in the music. Then is the time to say, "Good for you, John, nice jump." After the music stops, the teacher can say, "Children, something new has happened. John gave a fine jump with the music. Start the music back where John felt that jump. John, will you show us how you did it? Beautiful! Watch how he shoots straight up in the air, the string pulled very high. We do not jump with our feet, you see. The lift inside shoots us up in the air. Our legs just hang down like strings under us. If we keep our center pulled high, we can do beautiful things. We can even turn and whirl as we jump. There is nothing in our way.

"Now boys, line up over at the side and jump as your name is called."

"What a wonderful jump, Ming! I never get over being surprised how you children can do things when you just let go and are not afraid.

"Good, Rudolf. Another beautiful jumper. Watch the little bounce he gives at the end. He doesn't come down with stiff ankles to make the building shake. He comes down on cat's feet.

"Now let us play the record from the beginning and, when the music makes you feel like jumping, jump right where you are. If we all made a great run first it would be a pretty terrible mix-up. Fine, Manuel! Fine, José!

"Now the girls can have their turn."

So the children, through praise in pleasant association, start jumps and leaps which, as time goes on, will give them great satisfaction in their dancing.

Thumping Downward Drop

As the children's feeling for music grows, we will see them expressing it with ever-increasing variety of movement.

Although the "lift" is the primary movement, there is also in combination with it a thumping downward drop, coming from the center also. It is just like the downward fall of the ball. This we saw them use in the joggety part of the "Hungarian Rhapsody."

"Turkish March" (Victor Record No. 1196) bangs the children down on the floor, the sound of their feet making a staccato accompaniment. The boys especially love these downward, weighty movements.

Dropping Fold

Then there was the Dropping Fold we saw as the music died down in the "Hungarian Rhapsody." Some child will let her body drop a little, suggesting such a movement. Then the teacher can say, "Dolores just started to do something very beautiful. When the music died down she started to let herself drop down with it. I wonder if we could help her through with that beautiful movement. Try it again, Dolores. This time without stopping. Keep your center pulled high but let your knees and everything else soften. It is just as if you were pouring yourself down. As you go down, tuck yourself in under, bringing your knees forward as if you were sitting in a swing.

"Now she can pour herself up, pulling from the center. Keep that soft, poured feeling."

The Whirl

And then the whirl. The children love this and it is very beautiful. The whirl starts from way inside and corkscrews up and out, the arms flinging out from the center to balance.

After this corkscrew whirl is established, softening and dropping our head back will let the arms up higher till they can draw great circles in the air. Or the opposite. After the corkscrew turn is established, dropping the top part of us softly forward gives us a folding whirl.

Calling Names

Training the children to dance forward when they hear their names called is a means of strength for the teacher as well as adding great beauty to their dancing.

In this way the teacher is always in control. She can send the children forward or call them back. When the space is limited as in the schoolroom, it is almost necessary.

This calling of names gives a chance for solo dancing—then adding another and another until finally the teacher can call "Now everybody," and the whole room goes forward.

Having everyone dance during part of each record is good, even though it crowds the space for a time, because it gives every child his eagerly awaited turn and gives the more backward ones strength through numbers.

Emotional Index

The teacher will learn to judge her children more surely through their dancing. It can serve as an emotional index. For instance, I would never have known how very sensitive and self-conscious Mee Lee was, had I not watched her clinging close to the wall, like Chuchundra, the Muskrat, with never the courage to go out in the middle of the room. Here was a child, I saw, with whom I must use great sympathy and understanding.

Then there was Tommie, whose story is on page 136. He came to our room, took one look at all our Mexican and Chinese children, and told his mother, out loud for us to hear, "I don't like it here." He stayed, and the first day or two brought us such trouble in the yard that the children took him to task.

"Why did you sass two teachers in one day?" they asked.

"Why did you call the principal an old Sour Puss behind her back?"

"Because I felt like it," was the best thing Tommie would say.

The children were wild. "What if everybody did what they felt like doing?"

Time passed and things went better with Tommie, but not so with Ming Chan. So one day the children put him on the spot.

"Why did you hit Yoshiko?"

"Why did you coach Yon Lee to say 'Japanese people no good'?" they demanded of him.

"Because I wanted to," repeated poor Ming, making a weak show at defiance, although tears were running down his cheeks.

Then, joy of joys, who was it coming up in front to champion the cause of decency and fair play? It was Tommie, and he said, "Now Ming, remember how I talked back the first time I was up here, and I found it didn't do no good."

Oh happy moment for all of us! When recess bell rang, I stood at the door, shook his hand, and said, "From now on you're tops with me, Tommie."

So after recess, and this is the point I'm coming to, we danced. We had had a strenuous set-to over our international incident. But Tommie, instead of having to be coaxed to go up as usual and then skulking behind the others in furtive fashion, was marching up as though he belonged, and holding his head as high as anyone. And how he danced!

He had known what there was to know about this dancing before. It wasn't a question of knowledge or ability. He knew how and he was plenty bright. It was the emotional mix-up within him. His guilt feelings—his feeling that he wasn't really what we wanted—what we stood for in the room. That he had no right to dance was what had held him back.

Only as the teacher builds the child's own faith in himself is she building his dancing.

Congratulate Ourselves

Now let us go back to the beginning again.

At first we had a roomful of children embarrassed at the thought of dancing. We explained a bit of their fears away by telling them of this new kind of dancing that was for boys, girls, grown-ups, and everybody. "We don't go anywhere to learn it. It is inside ourselves. We just feel the music and let it come out our own way."

Then we stressed and have continued to stress the importance of the Body Lift—telling the children that they are like a puppet held high on a string. We bounced as if we had a rubber ball inside us and rocked forward as if we were pumping in a swing. We opened and closed like an accordion —expanding as we opened wide and folding as we closed.

Next we worked with the children to help them find that inner co-ordinated movement that starts at our Body Center and goes out. Our hands and feet grew heavy moving from the center. Our legs and neck grew long.

We learned to turn in the circle as we rocked forward and turn again as we folded back.

We, as teachers, learned to praise, praise, praise, especially as we saw it was needed.

Then we broke away from the circle, turning all about the room—filling all the space.

We began stressing the feeling tone more directly—testing the children with the beautifully quiet "Monastery Garden" and then the jolly "Grasshopper Dance."

We saw the beginnings of the child's innate response to the changes in music as we put these two moods together in "Dark Eyes" and "Two Guitars."

From here we watched the development of the jump and the thumping staccato movements, the whirl and the dropping fold.

We learned to call the children forward and back in tempo with the music. We found we could judge our children more surely emotionally.

We watched the children evolving from a few simple elements a free, spontaneous dancing, growing in emotional depth and sensitivity of expression.

Surely we have made a beginning, rather shaky, perhaps, but a beginning, nevertheless, that will lead us far into the beauties of children's dance expression.

If the teacher can't visualize the body movements as described here, she should not worry about it. Movement is very difficult to get from the printed word. She should forget the outer technique and concentrate on the Body Lift and freeing the children emotionally. If the children are freed, a simple skip about the room is a thing of joyous beauty. As the children feel the music they will find their own means of expressing it. As in their painting, it will spill out somehow. Each term she will find greater and greater surety. But this cannot come through courses or lectures on the subject. It must come through actual laboratory experience with the children.

Her room dancing, while being equally free, spontaneous, and sincerely beautiful, will have something of her own personal quality about it, making it utterly distinctive and different. She will gain satisfaction born of her own creative effort. Working with the children and marveling at their ability to create beautifully, she will go forward to great joy and satisfaction.

5. Creative Writing

I wanted free, creative expression in the children's writing. But how to go about it? I knew little or nothing about creative writing. What were the values? What were the criteria? Finally I decided I would worry no longer about the academic approach. That, I knew, would fail in art. Why would it not fail here? Fundamentally, weren't they the same anyway?

My roomful of fourth-grade children had taught me what was true in their art. Might they not lead me here? The child had sincerity, directness, and rhythm in his art—delightful emphasis and unexpectedness. "Why not take those as my criteria?" I cried excitedly. How simple it all became.

Gone was the insecure feeling that I had missed out on something academic and could never know intellectually how to judge their writing. I would "feel" my way. I would work to free the child and give him faith and confidence. He would open up as he did in his art. He would teach me.

I would accept the challenge of the children's limited background and opportunity. We would write of life about us. Relief and the County Visitor? Drunks and fights down the street? We would bring them into the schoolroom and by sharing experiences find relief and understanding.

How like an adventure it was becoming! This would be no tedious correcting-grammar-and-punctuation ordeal.

Grammar and punctuation could take a vacation if need be, or be brought into the picture later so casually as not to upset the emphasis. The writing must come as best it could and be accepted on its own merit for the thought, the feeling, the life force, the creative personal touch that it contained. Step by step we would learn free, glorious expression together.

The next morning a child told of a drunken woman asking his father to help her across the street. I remarked, "Well, of course this isn't just the kind of neighborhood any of us would choose to live in. But perhaps a place that is so bad is really very good, because it can teach us what is fine, and what isn't, in life. You won't grow up like some children, to think drinking is smart because they have never seen the suffering that comes from it. Maybe we could all begin thinking these things out in the back of our heads and write about them."

So we began.

The first writing was rather poor and lifeless. Many of the children wrote little or nothing at all. What could I do to give things a boost, a little more incentive? If I could only put their good writing up, as I did their pictures, where it could be seen by all and win recognition accordingly. Why not a newspaper?

Wall Newspaper

"Children, your writing is just as interesting as your pictures. I wish we could mount the best of it on the wall. But it's so little nobody could read it. . . . Now if we could write it large. . . ."

"Why not write it big and put it on the cupboard?" someone shouted.

Why not indeed? Fortunately there was a great row of

cupboards running nearly the length of one wall. There we would hang the large sheets as they were written.

Then, with the wall newspaper in mind, we wrote again about the neighborhood—"Street Scene" we called it. Over and over these first papers I went, feeling, testing them for honesty, for individuality of expression. Had someone made a reference to something in his own life which only he could tell? Was there a sentence or two that might suggest to my untried ear promise of a power and directness to come? Such sentences I encircled with colored pencil, meaning they could be copied on our newspaper. Many times my first markings were changed for better as my understanding grew. Trying hard to find something good from each child, I put these parts together in relation to each other to make a unified whole. Then I numbered them and put them away for the morrow.

Perhaps that sounds like a lot of work. It wasn't. Because at first, when I was stumbling to know what it was I was looking for, most of the children were only able to write very few, faltering sentences. Later, as they wrote better and longer, other people about me became interested. I would read them the chosen morsels, testing them orally on my own ear and theirs.

The next morning at school I listed the names on the blackboard in the order of their contributions, under "Newspaper Today." I watched the children search eagerly to see if their names were there.

When it was time to begin writing the newspaper, the first child went to the table and copied the encircled part from his story. This was an all-important moment. It meant that something he had written was found to be good and was needed for the newspaper.

Writing born of confidence and faith.

"Street Scene

His part, copied well or badly, brought praise or blame accordingly from his fellows. It was only natural, at first, that his hand would shake and many mistakes seemed bound to happen. Now when handwriting was discussed, there were few who were not ready and willing to accept pointers on how to make their writing better. Capitals and correct spelling you just had to have in a newspaper.

At first the children wrote very much the same. But as they saw that an idea could be chosen only once, they began to draw more and more from within themselves, bringing out individual bits that only they, with their own background of experience, could summon. Only in writing sincerely of their own experiences, thoughts and feelings were they assured a place in the sun—which was the wall newspaper.

And so was conceived our wall newspaper that was to give us joy and activity, and in the course of a year and a half, to develop our writing beyond all recognition.

This is the text of our first newspaper, as gleaned from several writing periods.

Street Scene

In our room we have very good intelligent people but by my house there are a lot of drunk men. There is a man called "The Snake." He sells liquor. One day he tried to make my father drunk. My mother said, "Don't be so dumb. We need the money for the rent." My mother says to my brothers, "I hope you won't get drunk when you are big."

Sometimes you get drunk and kill somebody. Next day you find yourself walking up thirty steps to the end of a rope.

At our hotel we do not let drunk people have a room, but they say they do not drink and bring company, and then they drink and bring company.

My lovely mother said to my sister, "If you are going to be a bad girl, I'll have to send you to a home." I said, "When I grow up I want to be a nice girl."

If I see a liquor store, I just feel like breaking the store down. I hate to see it. I hate to smell it. I just say to myself, "Why did they have such things?"

When my mother and I went down the street we passed a beer parlor. We saw an old drunk lady. She was older than my grandmother. My mother said, "How would you like to see your grandmother come out of there?" I said, "I would turn grandmother right over my knee and spank her, just like she does me."

Here the children's use of direct questions, and conversations—"I just say to myself,"—were already suggesting a show of freedom—of that unfolding from within. Just as there was rhythm through repetition in painting, just so, "I hate to see it. I hate to smell it," was giving rhythm here.

I felt a growing power within me to judge their writing. I began to respond more readily to their bits of charm and candor. It became easier and easier to choose a fresh sentence from a very limited child, or a good paragraph from a more able one.

I found that it made little difference to the child if his chosen contribution was only a line or two. He was undeniably part of the newspaper. And as the teacher said, "Sometimes one sentence will say more than a whole page." The child who was absent would ask if he could write his story the next day. He felt the newspaper needed his contribution and would suffer its lack.

I soon discovered the children who could take my place in overseeing each child as his copying time came. One of these children we made chairman each time, and it was his job to help the child writing to keep his place, remember corrections in spelling, capitals, and so forth. This relieved me of much tedium in that connection and also provided recognition for those children found able.

The writing of the newspaper was done with long-handled, stiff brush and ink. Sometimes it looked pretty bad. It was a question pedagogically if bad handwriting should be put up for all to see. I noticed this feature bothered visiting grown-ups. "Wouldn't it be better to have the best writers write for everyone?"

I could see their point. But this story-writing was to be born of giving confidence and faith. Wouldn't there be a happier, more equable feeling in the room if each child could copy his own story and have his best writing—for him—accepted kindly?

Once trying to get a child whose writing was almost illegible to relinquish voluntarily his right to a more able brushman convinced me that this right to copy the fruit of his own brain meant a great deal to the child. The child's fallen expression seemed to suggest suspicion that my whole support might be a hoax; that next his right to write a story might be taken away in favor of another.

"As time goes on we will improve," I assured people.

The writing did improve, but how much I did not realize until I went back to look at the first newspapers.

Giving Action

This writing at the newspaper table, with writer and chairman, and actually several other kibitzers who couldn't be driven to their seats, went on most of the day. However, I hasten to say that this did not take place every day. We were lucky if we got out one newspaper a week. When there was a discussion bringing up something of special interest, the children wrote. At the beginning it took the best from several such writing periods to make material for one newspaper.

During the writing of the newspaper the children going to write in their turn and the chairman slipping over to consult with me undeniably distracted attention from other activities. However, this was giving action to the room. All that was needed was that I should adjust myself to the going and coming, the reaching and hanging. And that, fortunately, I had pledged myself to do.

Everything the children did was reflected in their newspaper. So we find a child writing after a trip to the zoo:

Just think of meeting a tiger or a lion on a jungle night and you have no gun and you started to climb a tree. There were apes up in the tree and you have no way to turn. This tiger or lion eats you for hamburgers. But that won't happen here unless the animals break loose, I hope, I hope, I hope.

Another writes of his Tortilla Factory picture:

When I painted my picture, I thought I was making it funny. I put, "I like tortillas because they have no bones." But the teacher liked it.

The County Visitor

Facing the County Visitor frankly helps to take out the sting. Her picture mounted round the wall makes the children believe that she is nothing to be ashamed of, kept secret within. The fact that the teacher knows about her existence makes for a closer bond between them. So they wrote:

We have no visitor but we have trouble to keep a roof overhead and have gas and lights and to eat. I knew an old lady that had a visitor. One day the visitor said, "If I am going to help you, your son must not work." But the old lady did not mind. So one day the visitor found out her son was working and stopped helping her. She got so mad she said if the President of the United States was here she would tell him.

They told us they can't help us because we have to complete a year. Then my father got a little job, and it help us a lot, but still we need four more months.

I suppose you think why my father don't work. But he does. He gets work once a week or two times a week. You may guess the rest.

I found myself learning more about these children and their lives than I could hope to learn in years in any other way. For the children wrote:

One day a man called to me and said, "Do you want some candy?" I told my mother and she said, "Did you take the candy, Shirley?" And I said "I am not so dumb as you think I am mother."

One day a man called to me to give me some money, but I didn't pay any attention to him. I walked into an apartment house like as if I lived there.

Through sharing these experiences with the group, and discussing them, the children were freed of the unwholesomeness attending their suppression. The children could see that such experiences were common to the group and were no reflection on the individual.

A Joyous Experience

Little by little writing became as fascinating as painting. Many more children were being afforded recognition for work well done. Now there was a reason for handwriting and spelling and punctuation. Writing was becoming a live, joyous experience, both for the children and the teacher.

First there was the joy of expressing their own thoughts and experiences. Then came the satisfaction of seeing one's name listed on the board as an important contributing member of the group. Each child watched with hawklike eyes as name after name was crossed off and his own grew near for action.

Then came the writing with brush and ink, with the chairman's eyes upon him. Each child summoned all his wits and body control to win approbation and respect. If things did go wrong, there was always the teacher to stick up for him—to give him faith that next time would go better.

After each page was finished and thumbtacked to the wall, every child could feast his eyes on his own work.

Communal Reading

Then came another angle—the communal reading aloud of the newspaper.

"In this room we write stories from inside ourselves," someone explained to the children from the room across the hall. "Everyone writes his own way. It is more fun this way."

"Then," someone else took it up, "we copy it on our newspaper. We try to copy it good. We write it on the little paper, then we put it on the big."

During the reading the chairman, or the best writer, or the one who had contributed the best story, or whose mother was visiting, or whose birthday it was, stood alongside and kept place with a pointer.

"Be ready—your turn, and no sleepy head," she cautioned.

Then the reading began. Each child waited his turn, his moment of recognition. Child after child rose with hardly a break in continuity, to read, with assumed modesty, his contribution. English, broken into all sorts of bits—Mexican, Chinese, Japanese, and illiterate American, but read with self-respect and confidence. Even when correction had been made, the importance of the occasion would, as often as not, make it come out the funny way it was written on the original little paper.

The group responsibility to see that every child got on his feet on time bespoke a mass interest, a feeling of belonging. The variety of the children and their voices coming from here and there all over the room made as effective and dramatic an occasion as one could hope to experience.

The wall newspaper presented concrete evidence to the children that the room was doing something. So great was their interest that the children remembered who wrote each part from one end of the year to the other.

Punctuation Marks

Now a word about punctuation marks. As we get older our senses are liable to become dulled, constrained, anxious about the form rather than the substance. Just as children's painting cannot be judged by adult standards, so children's creative writing cannot be judged by such things as punctuation and sentence structure. These must be built up gradually over a long period of time.

I remember when I was a child. With what joy the teacher jumped all over the paper, putting in punctuation marks! In this way she could vindicate herself . . . it was her excuse for being. It kept before our minds constantly the fact that she was superior. No matter what we would write, she could always find something wrong. It kept us in our proper place. How kind that teacher would have been if once she had praised the content rather than correcting the form.

If we wish to get live, creative writing from children we must see this whole thing in its proper perspective. If the teacher puts too great emphasis and value on question marks and quotation marks, the child's questions will dry up at their source and his quotations fail to happen.

When we feel we must give attention to punctuation, why not take a bit from some child's story and put it on the board and stress its strength and beauty? Then say casually, "There are a few things we could do to this that would make it a little easier to read, but they are not the important things."

Someone will say, "Quotation marks around so and so."

"Yes, not that your story won't be good without quotation marks. I can imagine a whole page just covered with quotation marks and it wouldn't be any good at all." The children laugh.

"But if you can remember to put them around the exact words people say, it will help others to read it correctly. But if it will bother you too much in thinking of fine things to say, forget the quotation marks."

Now ten to one next time there will be a show, at least, of quotation marks. A few when praised will beget others. And the whole question of quotation marks will come as easily as breathing because there is no fear.

Spelling

If the child must spell all his own words, his ideas are curbed, if not blocked completely. So the teacher divides her time between going about encouraging the children and writing words for them on the blackboard. This spelling of the children's words puts no limit on what they can say. They can soar as high as they please. Children who have been held back by the want of knowledge of how to spell the simplest words will blossom forth like magic. When the children see the teacher at the board, they know it is again "word time."

A little girl from the back of the room calls, "Hemden-hawd."

"I'm sorry," says the teacher.

"Hemdenhawd," the child says again.

"I'm sure it's a very good word," says the teacher, praying for light. The child comes forward and says, "Hemden-hawd. My grandmother hemmed and hawed."

When a child calls for an especially good word, the teacher draws a circle around it to show it is deserving of praise and recognition.

At the end of the writing time, the teacher says, "Time to choose for our 'Story Word Book.'" The children choose words while the teacher underlines on the board. As more and more words go into the word book, the children need ask for fewer and fewer. The spelling lessons follow naturally from these words asked for and chosen by the children.

Cues from the Child

Now more about the actual conduct of the story writing. First the teacher will want to attune herself to what is of interest and meaning to the children. She will take her cue from them.

Let us suppose it is the first week of school. A child confides, "When I was a baby I wouldn't go on the merry-go-round because I thought it was an animal."

"Is that true?" says the teacher. "I can understand how a tiny child would feel that way."

Another edges in:

"When I was a baby we lived at San Pedro. Whenever the fog whistle blew I would cry and be afraid."

"That's very interesting too," says the teacher. "That can give us an idea. I believe nearly all of you have something you could tell about yourselves when you were little. Things you were afraid of, funny things you said and did, maybe a time you ran away. Stories your mother or someone else has told you. Why not let us write about them—just anything we can remember. Write it your own way. Don't worry about it."

The teacher goes about encouraging the children, convincing them that what they write is of interest to her and assuring them that they can write well if only they let go and are not afraid.

She praises the poor faltering sentence of the slow child, reading it aloud as she praises to show that she can read it with perfect ease.

And indeed the teacher is interested. For from each writing lesson will come her own growth and her own surety. And indeed the children will write well when they let go and are not afraid.

What do the children write this day? Nothing very wonderful. Perhaps the most interesting story is:

Once when I was little I was in the show and I pull a man's wig. Then I said to my mother, "I have pull his hair off and it did not hurt him." Then my mother said that it was not his hair but it was his wig. Then I thought she meant it was some kind of animal and I ran out of the show and begin to cry.

But the teacher is getting the child to express himself from his own background of experience and is developing his respect for himself as a personality of interest. Also she is gaining a little significant information that will aid her in understanding this child in particular, and all children in general. If the teacher is interested in what John said or did when he was a baby, she is helping to establish a friendly feeling, a rapport between them that will make her every word count. Don't we ourselves like people who are interested in us as human beings rather than what we know of Holland, airplanes, or anything else?

Spooky Stories

A story with a spooky element is told at news period. Hands begin waving to tell other such stories. All right, relax. Let the children write about them. When they are interested, they will write easily. Children learn to write by writing.

One child writes:

When my grandmother was asleep one night she heard somebody calling. She got up and went to the door but nobody was there. Then she heard a voice telling her that a snake was in the baby's bed. And my grandmother killed the snake and the one that was telling her was my grandfather who was killed in the mines and that baby was my mother.

An interesting story if you're not fussy and afraid! And think what an eager, writing period! Such stories play a big part in the folk background of these children. How much closer they will feel to the teacher if they find she is interested too.

Later the children themselves will recognize these writing opportunities and we will have a child speaking out as in "All Worn Out Before Breakfast." (page 125.)

"The Deeper You Dig"

A teacher can remember choice ideas the children have expressed and make reference to them throughout the year. In this way the children gain the same respect for their ideas that they do for their painting.

I remember once speaking with the children about those who stopped writing, feeling they had written all they could, when perhaps the very next thing would have been their best.

Roberto said, "Sure, the deeper you dig, the better ideas you get."

All through the term we would play on that. "Anyone can write the easy things on top, but what is it Roberto says, children?" And the children would shout, "The deeper you dig!"

Roberto's mother had died and he hadn't much to be proud of.

Feeling and Imagination

Near the end of the second term writing full of feeling and imagination from the children's own background of experience began to pour out.

Ofelia, a ten-year-old Mexican child wrote:

. . . . Sunday the moment I got there I couldn't keep my eyes on anything but the Holy Mother holding the baby. I thought, "She's alive. Look," I said to myself, "look at her; she's calling me to come and pray."

In another mood she wrote:

Now the other morning Roberto came along when I was painting in the middle floor, and spilled my water all over my picture. I got so mad I almost saw the devil. I was thinking that my hair turned into some horns. I was seeing sights—devils all around me were pulling me with their great big forks of fire and I was trembling. Just what would you do if someone spilled water on your picture? Just what would you do?

A tiny Filipino boy wrote on Mother's Day:

. . . . Then my mother got a job in the nut factory. She was gone from seven in the morning until seven at night. Gee, I remember how tough it was to just have a mother at night and every morning. I was only five years old, but every night we had supper ready. My brother was just three years old but I told him what to do to help me. When he didn't want to, I said, "Don't you want mama to eat?" And he'd say, "Yes." So he helped me.

Alicia wrote of the plaza near by:

There at the plaza men drink their wine where their wives cannot beat them with a rolling pin. There they cannot be bothered by no one. Across the plaza stands Olvera Street where they can go and eat tamales. On Mexican holidays almost all the drunk men gather around and rejoice the holiday. Lots of old men or young men go and talk all about religion. Sometimes men go and make speeches about the poor people and that annoys the rich people. I admit that the plaza is not a healthy place to stay. Some men borrow money, and believe me or not they do not pay a penny back and say tomorrow—"mañana."

It's fun for the teacher to get stories from other sources:

When I was at Chinese school the teacher told us about a very poor boy. He lived in an old house without any light. He like to read book and he live by hisself. His mother and father die. Every night he go to a crack in his house to read the book. The crack open to the other house. When they go to sleep he cannot read the book.

If she is an enthusiast for correlating everything with arithmetic, this may please her:

I heard of a man in China that he's 95 year old, and every day he go out to his farm and pick some rice. Every day he bring two bag out. Each bag was full and each bag was 60 pound. 60 and 60 make 120 pound. He carry each bag one on the right hand and the other bag on the left hand. I think that old man was real strong.

A little boy, lately come from China, pushed his way through the difficulties of a foreign language to write because the subject was vital to him:

Thursday morning the Chinese Association say every Chinese go to Long Beach to stop the Japanese ship before he take the scrap iron. On Friday and Saturday morning four bus was wait to go to Long Beach at 8 o'clock and four bus was wait to go at 10 o'clock. Now I will tell you the story. What the scrap iron is used for. They hit the scrap iron to pieces and they put the scrap iron pieces in the bomb and they go up the sky and drop the bomb. The scrap iron pieces come out of the bomb and hit the people.

Now we want to stop them. You know how many scrap iron in Long Beach? Thirty ton!

Little Francisco would have a difficult time writing about transportation or foods or any number of things, yet he wrote this, to wring one's heart:

. . . . They put a record about birds, a happy song, and then six men took the box. It was a pretty box. . . . I wish I have my mother. She used to tell me, "Be a good boy" when I was at the hospital. When she was at the hospital she used to say, "My little children." . . . I could not eat without her.

Happy Days Are Here Again

It is our job to help the children to start writing about something that is near and meaningful to them. The first day of school is a subject that has meaning for all children. It is the beginning of the third semester. Notice the ease, the rhythm and the feeling with which they write.

Last night my sister Jessie said, "Put the alarm and put the time so tomorrow I can get up early in the morning." I said, "All right, but I don't need an alarm to wake me to go to school. Not on your life. I am too excited to get to school and hear the old magic word, 'Children. . . .'"

Last night when I was in bed already and not asleep yet I told my mother, "I wish tomorrow would come quick." My mother said,

"Well, go to sleep and you won't feel nothing." I went to sleep and this morning as soon as I opened one eye I didn't wait another minute. I jumped out of bed toes first. . . .

School is a happy, jolly thing. I like school because we can learn a lot of things. If you are at home you do not learn nothing but just sitting down.

While I was putting on my shoe and stocking I kept saying, "School again! School again!" I jumped up and washed my face and hand. I dried my face and it got clean for another day that starts our happiness—that means at school.

Cannot Go by Clock

Creative writing cannot go by the clock any more than creative painting can. It cannot be confined to a twenty- or thirty-minute period. Usually the children write as long as they have something to say. There is always a ragged end when some have written all they can and others are still hard at work.

Howard, who became our Comedy Dancer, started writing about the circus. He wrote on and on straight through recess time, the children according him respect for his interest.

Speedy light and cloudy dust—make way, for here comes Silver, carrying latest story from Room 13.

Once when we went to the circus and we seen a fat lady that weighed 745 pounds and I just wondered how it felt to be that fat, and I said to my mother, "How would you like to be that fat?" And she said, "I don't think I would like it very much." And we seen the skinniest man in the world and the fattest man in the world and the tallest man in the world and the smallest midgets in the world. We seen the monkey lady and she was real funny. She looked like a monkey. And the fattest man weighed 445 pounds and the tallest man in the world was 16 feet high. We seen a lady that let snakes crawl on her and I thought it might bite her but it never. And we seen a man that would burn fire in his hand and the man with two mouths. He had a mouth in his face and a mouth under his wing bone. And we seen the lady with the iron tongue and she could hook a chain in her tongue and on the other end of her tongue was a twelve pound cannon and she held it off the floor with her tongue and shot a shot gun shell out of the cannon. And then we seen the half man and the half woman, but I never got to see it.

We seen the man that could swallow swords and we seen the man that fought a alligator and the alligator was wild too. And we seen the lady that was only half there and still alive and we seen the girl in the fish bowl and she could stay there fifteen minutes.

And we rode the electric cars and the merry-go-round and the ferris wheel and I bought some of the flavored ice and I rode the ponies. . . . And we shot guns and threw balls and shot sling shots and had a lot of fun. And they sold the best ice cream at the circus that I ever ate in my whole life, unless it was when I was a little baby and I can't remember.

Well, so long, nice dreams.

And I like to write and that is why I have written such a long story.

Next morning I read the story out loud quickly, all in one gulp. The children liked it. It was rather amusing that Howard, after having invented most of the story from his wishful thinking, should have strained his conscience over the ice cream. When I saw him alone I smiled at him and asked casually, "Did you really do some of those things, Howard, or is it all just a make-believe story?"

"Oh sure," he said, hunching his shoulders in a nervous way he had. "I did some of 'em, not all of them, but some of 'em."

English broken into bits, but read with self-respect and confidence.

Now the children illustrate their own stor

Movies

Why not let them write about the movies? Here we have their interest surely. Take these excerpts from one child's story for instance:

There in the castle was a coach ready, and the driver was Dracula and done him big eyes like a cat and the man got scared, but he went on. . . .

The coach started to go fast, and the man said, "Slow down, driver," and there was no driver there, but there was a bat in front of the horses. . . .

Then they were going up the stairs and there was a lot of webs of a spider, and Dracula went right through them, but the man had to take his cane and break them. And the bats were saying, "Boo, boo, boo," and then Dracula said, "What beautiful songs they know, and every night they sing for us—they sing for us, yes." . . .

But meanwhile the crazy man was in a crazy house and was trying to get out, and he ate flies and said, "Why do I eat flies when I can get nice, juicy spiders?"

We understand this boy better if we know what movies he likes:

Well, as I was saying, my fine feathered friend. I saw a picture that I didn't like. All I hear is, "I love you," and "My sweet, you're wonderful." They were in romance. All I like is pictures of gangsters and cowboys and not love things. . . . That's all I can tell you folks. See you next year.

Sometimes it is an inkling of how the one-third is thinking:

I saw a picture about the Dead End Kids. They were poor and there was a boy that lived near them and he was rich. One morning the rich boy went to the garden to eat his breakfast, and he had to drink milk. He didn't like milk so he took his milk and poured it in a flower pot.

When I saw that he did it, I thought he should have given it to the Dead End Kids. So the richer they get, the stingier they get. When they have something they don't want, they throw it instead of giving it to poor people. The rich people they have big cars and they have chauffeurs to drive the cars. The rich people sit and when the chauffeur goes fast they say to slow down. Then the chauffeur says, "Who is driving?" Then they fire him.

For These Things

By November many of the children are writing long stories and it is difficult indeed to know where to cut. This next story is written by a Japanese child:

My mother said when she was looking at the sun, "How marvelous to have a sun. It's good for everybody in the whole world." And she continued, saying, "How beautiful the moon is, and everything, and how peaceful this world is."

I was listening to her saying that and tears almost came down. This time I continued. I said, "No, you mean thankful to God that made our life and made the world."

My mother told me, "How thankful to see you walk and run." Because my mother told me even when I was three or four, I couldn't walk, and my mother was worried and thought I would not walk all my life. Finally one day I came walking to my mother. My mother took a long breath and said, "How thankful!" And she said it again. Everytime she was talking about it she would take a deep breath. She would say, "What close shaves and how lucky life." My father would interrupt and say, "If that luck didn't come to us, we would be pulling you in a wagon and you wouldn't play and jump."

I said, "How did you know that I wouldn't walk for life?" He said that the doctor told us, but it wasn't true.

Bits from children's stories follow:

I am thankful I have my mother for my father was blowed up in the mine. I get 2 thousand 400 when I'm 21. I'm thankful I'm not back in Kentucky where the snow is waist deep.

I am thankful for my mother and I think my mother is thankful for me and for the doctor that brought me through. And boy did I have a lot of hard bumps coming but got here safe. And are they thankful for the incubator that they put me in! . . .

Notice the power and rhythm as this next child writes:

When you look out of doors, or when you are there, you see all the beauty of the world. You see the sea, the beautiful waves that curl as they come. You see the beauty of flowers, of trees that give shade and that decorate our beautiful world. . . .

Some of you don't know the world! You do not notice it. You do not notice the beauty of the world! You do not notice the wonderful things that make you grow strong and healthy. If you would notice all these things, then you would know the world and enjoy life better.

The next is from the child who starts her story in the newspaper picture with a breezy, "Well, well, well."

The ocean is such a beautiful thing I sure am thankful for it. When the tide comes beating in on the rocks, and you see white caps breaking, the moonlight shining on the ocean and the beautiful colors—that beautiful bluish green, the fish that swim all the time and the plants that grow at the bottom of the sea and the wonderful sea bottom animals and the beautiful clams and the beautiful sea-weed, you don't think of it until you sit down and realize about it. Everything is beautiful.

Now I will tell about the earth—what's beautiful on the earth. Well, here I go. The earth is simply marvelous—the trees, for instance. Just think about them. Now the pepper tree. The leaf is different than any other leaf. Have you ever picked a pepper leaf? And their smell is so different, and the little red pepper that comes on it. . . . Everybody should be thankful for our beautiful earth. . . .

I am thankful that I get free lunch and cod-liver oil. I like the free lunch because they give different kinds of food and at my house we just eat beans and when there is nothing to eat we eat nothing. We are thankful with just beans.

We Write about Christmas

Children are always interested in Christmas. As we give the children a respect for honesty and sincerity in their writing we get the following:

Santa Claus in the Hospital

I told my mother all I like to have for Christmas, so she said she didn't think Santa Claus could get around with that much. She said he break his back with so much.

My mother told me when she was little and Christmas came along, my mother ask her mother if Santa Claus was coming down the chimney that night. Then her mother told her that Santa Claus was in the hospital. Then mother was so sad, so when her father came home she told him that Santa Claus was in the hospital for a long time but she can wait till he get out of the hospital and come to see her and bring her some toys to play with, to pass the time away with happiness. She said she hope everybody will be happy on Christmas.

The next child, a Mexican, is the youngest of five girls. The mother dresses them all and keeps them in school on the little wages the father earns as bus boy at a big hotel.

Christmas Does Not Mean Nothing to My Family

We pass it like it was a week day. The only thing I got last Christmas, a lady gave me a doll that have been broken—a doll that have been used.

Some people has presents and has brand new dolls. They all go out and play with their dolls, and I feel so sad. And they ask me, "What did you get?" I just go in my house and begin to cry. And my mother said, "What is bothering you, Christmas? I wonder who invented Christmas."

My mother told me about when she was little that after her mother died when Christmas came the only thing she got was a little jar with 5¢ in it. She used to think she had a million dollars.

But after her father died she live with a mean lady and she did not have any Christmas. And I begin to cry inside myself, and I kiss her.

1—2—3—Hurray for Christmas!

In Christmas I don't want my mother to give me gifts. I want to give her, instead of she giving me.

Even if I don't get no toys in Christmas like other boys and girls, I am happy because it is the day that Christ was born. I feel sorry for some poor people which haven't any home to live and have to go begging for a place to sleep and to live. I'm glad I have ten dollars and 91 cents so if some day I am sick and my mother or father haven't any money for the doctor, all I have to do is go to the bank and say, "Give me $10.91¢." I show them my bank book and they tell me, "Sign here." Then I sign and I go home and tell my mother, "Call the doctor. I will pay the bill." . . . 1—2—3—Hurray for Christmas!

Values

Stressing social values is the most important work of the teacher today. What the child expresses orally or puts in writing becomes part of him, especially as he receives praise and recognition for it. Attitudes toward society and work and family are the deciding factors in the life of the individual. These we must effect early. They are infinitely more important than any abstract subject could ever be. A morning spent dealing with a problem in honesty or kindliness or responsibility is spent in the best "activity" in the world.

It is near the end of the first year together. The children are writing their "Report Cards" which really means, of course, that we are all taking time off to consider our room values—the things we have been stressing as making for "the good life."

Various ones write as follows:

Our room don't have to hit people and make them quiet. Our room get quiet by itself. We don't put them in the corner and put a dumb hat on them. Our room "feel" the way it should be.

I am proud I am a Safety. If there weren't any Safeties the school would be awful. The children would be throwing paper and squirting water. The children would fight and balls would be all around the school yard.

Our teacher doesn't want us to be sitting down just like old men. She wants us to be bright and thinking what we are to do. We don't want a jail house with children sitting in the corner because we don't like it that way, that's why. But we have to help because one poor teacher cannot do it all.

Children should act like human, they are not animal. For instance, monkeys are always swinging from tree to tree and that's the way some children are just going from sit to sit bothering other people.

What a lot of longing this child must have been through before she could write: "For now I have learned and learned, so I can help too." Notice the build-up from the very beginning leading to this one sentence.

. . . . We want a room who is dependable all the time and help to each other. Some of the children are very good and do want help from other children. But some of the children do not want help from other children. They say, "We can help ourself. We do not need help from you—go away. I do not want you to help me. Shoo-fly, get away."

We do not want to be lazy. Tell someone to help you with what you are doing. Do not stay where you are and do not learn. When I was eight years old I did not know anything because my mind wasn't helping me to do my work. But after I got older my mind did make me work a lot. For now I have learned and learned so I can help too.

With what pride and importance one Chinese child adopted another little fellow who knew no English.

. . . . When we have arithmetic I always go to Yon Lee's desk and say, "Arithmetic, Yon Lee," and he says, "Oh boy!" When Yon Lee don't know things, I teach him.

. . . . Last term we wrote our own report cards too. I wrote that teachers are not mind readers. They do not know what is inside us. That's why we have to write our own report cards.

And may I present this as an educational gem written by one of the most limited children in the room.

In the other school I could not learn and in this school I know all right all the time. I have more fun in school than in the other one I used to go to, because I know how more times.

A teacher will find that freeing the child for art, dancing, and writing will also at the same time be freeing him for his arithmetic and other studies. The fact that a child has come from a room where much time and emphasis has been put on arithmetic does not necessarily mean that the child has been learning in like degree. As in his dancing he must be without fear and embarrassment before even his arithmetic learning can function properly.

Worries

It is important that we, as teachers, treat the whole child. We no longer neglect to feed him if he comes hungry. We see that his feet get dry on wet days. If a child is sick, we know he must get well before we can hope to teach him. But there are emotional difficulties more undermining than physical upsets. If a child is worried we must also treat the worry. And worries are not confined to the underprivileged.

When children are encouraged to write that which has real meaning, they find release from what is bothering them. Let me tell the story about little Japanese Yoshiko, who was mentioned in the dancing chapter. From being very capable she suddenly changed and contributed little to the group. At story-writing time she handed in her paper with next to nothing on it. Then it was discovered that Ming Chan and little Yon Lee had been bothering her. Yoshiko hadn't complained. She had just closed up. The teasing was stopped. Yoshiko, much relieved, wrote page after page at writing time:

Today we are writing our own report cards. We must be intelligent, wide-awake, kind, and loving to learn things. When people are mean to you, or are not kind to you, just ignore them, but be as kind as you could be. We should not think we are the smartest one, but think you are learning every day. No one is too smart; even the best one in the world will be dumb sometime. We should be dependable and obedient. . . . I try to be as kind as I could, but I do not be kind to people that are mean to me. But I should be kind to them and just ignore, but when people hit me or call me names I like to hit them back or call them back. Some children thinks I am a Chinese and the Mexicans call me "China," but I am not. Lots of people know I am a Japanese and call me "Jap," but I do not like it. Sometimes they hit me and call me names, but I can't help it if I am a Japanese or Chinese or Mexican, Korean, or any kind of nationality. So I can't stop the war in China, because I did not start it, and I don't like war, but I don't care if they are warring, just so I am not in it. . . . The old man who works for my father, he tells me he had some experience and tells me what to do and what I shouldn't. Every time I bring my paper home I show it to him, then he says, "Good." And he says I write better than he could, and he says, "You write like my wife did, but she's dead now."

He says that he thinks about his wife when he sees my writing. He said, "Your sister writes good but too small." He hisself used to write good but now he writes like this: "J. A. Trupp," that is his name. . . . That man was at the gambling house when his wife died and his girl could not do anything. . . .

This had been as clear a case of emotional blocking as one could hope to see. How would Yoshiko have fared in an intelligence test during this troubled period? How many times is seeming stupidity only a symptom of some very real worry in the life of the child?

Notice, too, the influence of a chance old man in the life of this child, filling a hunger for recognition and appreciation.

All Worn Out before Breakfast

I remember very well how these next stories came about.

"Boy, oh boy!" said Donna. "We sure had an argument at our house this morning. My father was shouting, 'Why, oh why do I have to have such a hateful son?' And my brother was yelling, 'Why can't we live like other famlies?' "

"That was a lovely family argument," said the teacher, all unimpressed.

"We have them lovely at our house too," said Anita.

"If a family didn't argue it would be sick—or maybe dead, huh?" she mused out loud.

"The interesting thing," continued the teacher, half to herself, "is to try to figure out why we're arguing. Donna's big brother, for instance—he's probably on edge because he can't find work and has to hang around the house and ask for a nickel. No wonder his father thinks he's hateful sometimes. He hates himself for not having work."

"Sure, her brother is good. He just want work, huh? My father didn't hit us when he have work."

"But my brother is mean," said Betty-Jo. "I put my

madonna up where everybody could see it. He told my father, 'Betty-Jo has a crocodile on the wall.' "

"He's jealous. Like my big sister. When I brought home my clay horse she said, 'Where did you get that rat?' "

"My mother always says, 'I wish you children wouldn't fight or quarrel, cause it worries me and I get tired listening.' She says, 'All you do is "Give me it—I won't"—and so on. Then you start to hit.'

" 'Sure,' I tell my mother, 'I can't help it, because my brother always start it.' Then he say, 'I do not—you do.' Then I say 'I do not—you do.' Then my mother says, 'Let's have peace in this house.' "

"My mother says," spoke up José, " 'All you do is worry me and wear me down.' "

"Sometimes we're all worn out before breakfast," said the one towhead. That's a good idea! Why don't we write 'All Worn Out Before Breakfast,' about, you know, all the arguments at our house?"

"How many think it's a good idea?" said the teacher. So off they went, with a live subject, finding relief in the fact that their teacher was not pained or shocked to hear, but understood and could find good where everything seemed bad.

Then the teacher asked, "Are there any more good titles?" As the children suggested them, she wrote them on the board.

"Quarrel, Quarrel, Quarrel."

"Why Can't We Live Like Other Families?"

"Quarrels, and Why."

"War, War, War in Europe and War at Home."

Now, after more than a year, there was much less call for spelling words. The children had learned many words through repetition in pleasant association. But let us see what they were writing.

A Chinese boy wrote:

In the morning my grandmother tell me to go buy something. I say, "Why don't you tell my brother?" Then my grandmother say, "You always eat it, don't you?" I say, "Yes." She say, "Then why don't you go buy it?"

"That's a grandmother with spirit," said the teacher admiringly.

And another:

. . . . And my mother always says, "I wish there was a hundred bathrooms so each person could go into them to clean theirselves without fighting."

Joe Chee, in his second year from China, has become American enough to write:

We fight over the radio. My brother tell me to turn to the music. I say, "No, I like to hear Dick Tracy." My brother say, "I like to hear the music." And he turn to KRKD, but I turn back to KHJ. Then he turn again to KRKD and I turn to KHJ. We turn and we turn to make the radio break and nobody hear the music or Dick Tracy, and we have to take it to the radio man to fix for $1.50.

The little fellow who wrote "1—2—3—Hurray for Christmas!" wrote:

Why can't we live like other families is right. Always all the time we're arguing about something. Why can't there be peace in the house at least for a few minutes. But no, they're always quarreling. Quarreling, quarreling, just like everything. I also quarrel myself. If it is not with my sister you can't tell who it is? Well, my dear old grandma. Most all the time it is because I don't want to get up early enough for school, or because she always tells me, "When you come from school you go to be back door because I lock the front one and I lay down and rest and when you ring the door bell I have to get up."

I said "All right," but I forget all about it and so I ring it. She tell me, "What did I tell you?"

"I forgot."

"All right, but don't forget it next time."

I say "All right, I won't forget. I give you my word I won't."

"All right, but keep your word."

So that's the way we quarrel, me and my grandma.

A child from one of the very few Chinese families on relief wrote:

At the breakfast table we argue more. When my mother give me my breakfast, my little sisters say, "You gave Dora the biggest piece. Why don't you give us the biggest piece once in a while?"

Then my mother says, "The smallest children have to get the smallest piece."

Writing for Guidance

Toward the end of the third term I had in mind somehow to get the children to write of their own, very innermost difficulties—those things that caused them to feel inferior and ill at ease with themselves, and the world. So I began somewhat as follows:

"Grown people have funny ideas. I was just thinking how many of them think that children do not feel things. That the only time they hurt is when they fall down or are spanked. I remember that the things that hurt me most and made me most unhappy had nothing to do with falling down and getting hurt, or being spanked. They were the things that made me ashamed and made me feel that I was not as good as other people. Why I can even remember that I was ashamed because I had tow hair, hair white as

paper, like Corrine's. My mother always talked about people with beautiful black hair and dark eyes, like most of
you have. I didn't know that there was anybody in the
world that liked tow hair. People called me that little 'Tow-
headed Robinson girl' and I was ashamed. Now when I see
tow hair I think, 'How beautiful!' I was ashamed of my
very name, Natalie. Nobody else in town had the name
Natalie. I wanted a name like Frances or Elizabeth, as two
of the most popular little girls were named. When old ladies
at church would say to me kindly enough, 'What's your
name, little girl?' I would answer 'Natalie,' and they would
say 'Madalyne, Mattie, what did you say?' And I would
say it bravely again, and the answer was always the same,
'Well, I never heard of that name before,' and I was crushed
and ashamed."

As long as I felt I had the children's attention, I went
back into my feelings as a child. In many cases I know I was
touching on sensitive ground. Then I said, "I'm glad to tell
you about these things because some people say that when
you're brave and dig down under and tell about these things
that hurt, they don't hurt so much any more."

So I began, as though to think out loud—"I wonder . . .
no, I guess it's really too hard a thing to ask . . . but still we
already have written very bravely about ourselves and it
hasn't hurt anybody—in fact, it has helped because it has
made us all one family. Well, at any rate, I was wondering
if you could write things about yourselves that have made
you feel embarrassed and unhappy. If it is something that
you are brave enough to have us read out loud, you can write
'O. K. to read out loud' on it. If it is just for me, you can
write 'Just for Mrs. Cole.'" And I wrote them on the
board.

Then someone asked about the title and the children, very quiet and respectful, suggested:

"Secrets About Our Own Lives."

"True Stories About Ourselves."

Now the first day, as you can guess, some of the very ones that I had hoped most would take part were the ones who contributed the least. However, I could see that they were gradually being intrigued despite themselves, and when the children began explaining, "This is just for you" or "This you can read out loud"—they were sorry they were not in on it. The next day nearly everyone took part.

The third day I read the stories that were marked "O K. to read out loud," while the children guarded for me with great respect, those for me alone.

As I read the stories, I tried to interpret them, easing the sting as best I could. The stories for me alone I could not act upon so directly, but bore in mind till opportunity presented itself.

May I begin with a story of a child who seems to be getting help of a sort at home?

She writes in part:

I always wish I was as good as everybody else is. My mother always tells me they are no better than I am. My mother says I may think they are better than I am, but they are not. My mother said they don't come no better than me. She said they may be smarter, but not better. . . .

This next is written by a tiny Chinese boy named Willie Samm.

. . . . I don't like people who is teasing me, and lot of other thing, and I don't like the bedbug and don't like to stay home and I don't like people who call me skinnybone and Uncle Sam and dirty pig and a rat, and the worst they call me is a Jap.

Several children wrote of their embarrassment the first day at a new school. Evidently it is a very difficult time for a sensitive child, and one which the teacher would help relieve if she understood.

. . . . and I was ashamed and I didn't know any teachers or children. They just passed by me. They didn't even talk to me. When I went home I told my mother, "They don't kinda like me because they didn't even talk to me." About six days they were talking to me and were kind. Then I was happy again. I played with them and I played with Ernest and many others. I went home and told her, "I am friends with the boys."

This very sensitive Chinese girl carried, beside her own, the embarrassments for the less sensitive members of her family. She writes:

. . . . My sister has such a funny name, Sue York. Imagine, Sue isn't such a funny name, but York! The boys and girls call her New York and I get so ashamed. Besides that, she has to wear special shoes, and they look like boy's shoes. Girls and boys say, "Why do you wear boy's shoes?" Sue York says proudly, "These are not boy's shoes, they are special shoes." Sue York is proud of those shoes; they last long, but I hate for anyone to say they are boy's shoes. . . .

And from another Chinese girl:

I used to be ashamed of my family, even myself. My father, grandfather and grandmother doesn't know English. When somebody comes to our house my grandfather yell out in Chinese, "Who's there?" I am ashamed when they asked me who yelled out. . . .

Aiko, a very chunky Japanese child with beautiful wide cheeks, wrote:

Oh, how I wish I could dance good! Even if I don't, I keep dancing and the children laugh and say, "Look at that girl dance funny. She just swings her hands back and forth."

I remarked that I was surprised to hear that Aiko thought she didn't dance well, for I had always liked her dancing. Of course she didn't leap and whirl like Sarah, who used to be in our room, but then Sarah was skinny, as the boys said. But Aiko gave us the strong, heavy downward pull that was very beautiful and just as necessary.

After my talking about this, Aiko danced without her usual embarrassment and was one of the first to raise her hand each time to go forward. This was one of the first things that encouraged me to feel I was accomplishing something.

Now I knew José better—José who was supersensitive, hiding himself away in books. For he wrote:

One thing I do, I walk in my sleep. Well, Saturday my aunt came to visit. When it was night we went to bed. We went to sleep. Then I was walking in my sleep. I went to my aunt. I was talking in my sleep. She said, "Well, anyway, what's the matter with this house, talking to me in the middle of the night?" I was talking to her little boys. My aunt said, "What's the matter?" Then she pushed me and I woke up. When I saw that I was sitting on the bed I said, "What happened?" She said, "Well, you was talking to me." Then my uncle woke up. He said, "What's all the fuss about?" My aunt said, "Well, he woke me up—it ain't my fault." Then they were all fighting and then my mother and my step-father woke up. My aunt told her all about it. My mother said, "Oh, he always walks in his sleep." So we went to sleep again about one o'clock, but in the morning she told me all about it. That's what I told you.

Along with all the other things wrong about his life, José had the double cross to bear of walking and talking in his sleep—things that by themselves are sufficient to convince a sensitive child that he is peculiar—not like other boys. What a triumph for him to be able to confess, "I walk and talk in my sleep."

After reading his story I could bring up the subject and interpret it for his reassurance.

The next story was written by a quiet little fellow whose mother and father worked in a restaurant.

My mother and father don't quarrel in the morning; they quarrel at night, when they come from work. They first start to quarrel and then they start to fight. I'm in bed when that happens and boy, I cover my ears with my hands when they quarrel and fight. I get under the covers when they fight. When they fight I get scared. Sometimes I think they're going to hit me when they fight. Sometimes we have to move. When they fight my mother says, "Hit me and see what happens." Sometimes she says she'll call the cops. After they get through fighting, it looks like a cyclone struck it. Boy, the house is a mess. My mother tells my father to get out of the house, and he says, "I like to see you make me." Then my mother says, "I'll get out then," and she says, "Put on your coat and hat, Orlando." I put on my coat and hat and we start to go out. . . . Then my father runs after us and says, "I'll go then." That's all they do, fight, fight, fight, fight. Sometimes the landlord or landlady chase us out of the apartment and it's hard to find another.

No wonder Orlando never seemed able to focus his attention. He had said we might use his story. The next day he was absent. I presented his story to the children with sympathy, and said, "Now you know how badly I feel that I have been impatient with Orlando for not giving us attention."

"Sure," said Alicia, "he close his ears at home so he cannot hear the fight. Then when he come to school, he have his ears closed and he cannot hear the teacher."

"And the sad thing is," said the teacher, "it is often people who love each other best who fight the most."

"Sure," added the towhead. "In one of the papers I was

fixing for my birdcage bottom, it told about a man who said he killed his wife because he loved her."

"Yeah," said Alicia. "Why did they invent love, anyway? It causes so much trouble."

Cruz, who wrote "You don't know the world" begins a long story as follows:

A long time ago, when I was younger, we used to live in other places where they were picking cotton and live in tents. And that was when my mother suffered a whole lot. We didn't have our father; we didn't have him before we started to live like that. He wasn't so very good father anyway. He was always cranky and he used to fuss too much and other things . . . but just the same he was our father and we had love for him. . . .

Children have spent years building defenses. We must establish a rapport through kindliness and sympathetic interest and be patient. We can't expect children to give us their best until we prove we deserve it.

Because of the need to get things out of the child until there is no heartache and sting, there is a great therapeutic value attending their writing. Because the story means so much to the child, good writing will come strong and true.

Aiko writes:

My mother and the four of us were going in the church where my father lay dead in his coffin. Pretty soon no more people came in; then they started to line up. They were going up there to pray just a few words. We went up first. The Japanese people do their funeral a different way. It is hard to tell how they do it, so I will not tell you the way the Japanese people do it, but I will tell how sorry the people were. My mother was crying bitterly and my brother handed her a handkerchief, and she said in Japanese, "Frank, you are very kanshine." (This is the word I didn't know in English, but you will understand.) I tried not to let a tear fall over my cheek.

I tried, but I couldn't. When I looked back at the crowd, I saw our best friend sitting crying because our father was dead. My little brother sat beside me and said, "Aiko, tell Mama not to cry any more, please." So I told mama to don't cry, please don't.

After that they put the coffin with my father in a big, black car. The rest of the cars were in a long row. When we got there we went slowly on a dirt road, and then came to a big house with a cross on top. . . . Then we went in the house. There was a hole and a thing sticking up and they put the coffin in it and everybody was crying.

They gave us a bunch of roses and the priest started to read the Japanese prayer and slowly the coffin went down the hole. We threw the roses in on it. My mother was crying bitterly and so was our best friend. When we got home, she lay down and our friends came in and said they were very, very sorry.

Now we go to church and pray to him.

If I have another chance to write I will write about my life, starting from when I was a baby till right now.

Now whether the academicians would call this creative writing I don't know. But remember, we have evolved our own criteria. In the first place, Aiko's story is absolutely sincere. It is written from her own life experience. It has a beautiful feeling tone. And it has bits, at least, of power and beauty.

After I finished reading this story to the class, a little fellow said, "They're crying! Sniff, sniff."

"Well, why not?" said the teacher. "I'm crying too. We cry at movies, over things that aren't half so beautiful."

"And aren't true!" shouted someone.

"Bad Little Boy"

Maybe we would feel differently toward the "bad little boy in the room" if we could set him to writing. A whole newspaper given over to Tommie's "feature story" may give him just the self-respect that he needs.

My father has blood poison and has not worked since last November. First it was just a little cut, so he went rabbit hunting and got dirt in it. . . .

When my mother gets a letter from him she is afraid to open it because she thinks he might be in trouble. . . .

If his leg gets cut off he does not care about himself. He is thinking of us kids and mother. He said, "You will never know how much I worried about you until you have kids like me. If you had the responsibility that I have you would worry yourself to death." I did not know how much he has worried. Now I know how much a real father and mother has to worry about a son and daughter. . . .

Us kids have not only been holding our breath, but it is more than that. We have been hoping and hoping. . . .

But life has to be lived, and lived right, although with roses or with devils. You can't have both. You have to be on one side or the other side of the fence. That is an old saying. Old sayings are sometimes right. Don't you think so? If you don't, your head is no good. . . .

Nobody is perfect. They do not sleep on a bed of roses. They have to wake up and not be a king or queen that doesn't have trouble. Where do you get the idea the queen and king don't have troubles? They have troubles and lots of them. So do you, and don't say you don't.

It is a far cry from the writing of more than a year ago. Then it was difficult to find a few good sentences. Now the stories are so long and so personal we have almost eliminated the newspaper.

We cannot hope to hasten this type of writing. We must await the opening, unfolding process.

The teacher's role of interpreter—relieving the worries of her children—is a challenging one indeed.

In Conclusion

In conclusion the teacher will find that children's painting, clay work, design, dancing, and writing are all the same underneath. There is the same marvelous creative ability within the child and the same need of confidence and faith to set it free.

When children are engaged in what they love to do, the barriers are down. The teacher has access to the child within. It is the attitudes we instil that make our job worth while.

Only as we build the child through giving joy and faith and confidence are we building his creative arts. When there is joy and faith, there also is the good picture, or writing, or dance. It works like magic—the perfect formula.

Working with these fundamental premises the teacher will be evolving her own approach, her own means of presentation, contributing from her own background of teaching experience and understanding.

Through giving the children confidence, the teacher will gain confidence, through sharing their troubles her own heart will become lighter, through enriching their experience, she also will be enriched.